AFRICAN WORLD HISTORIES

Africanizing Democracies
1980–Present

AFRICAN WORLD HISTORIES

Series Editor:
Trevor R. Getz, San Francisco State University

African World Histories is a series of retellings of some of the most commonly discussed episodes of the African and global past from the perspectives of Africans who lived through them. Accessible yet scholarly, *African World Histories* gives students insights into African experiences and perspectives concerning many of the events and trends that are commonly discussed in the history classroom.

Titles in the Series

Published

Cosmopolitan Africa, 1700–1875
Trevor R. Getz, San Francisco State University

Colonial Africa, 1884–1994
Dennis Laumann, University of Memphis

Transatlantic Africa, 1440–1888
Kwasi Konadu, City University of New York, and Trevor Getz, San Francisco State University

Africanizing Democracies, 1980–Present
Alicia C. Decker, Purdue University, and Andrea L. Arrington, University of Arkansas

Forthcoming

Sovereignty and Struggle, 1945–1994
Jonathan T. Reynolds, Northern Kentucky University

Bantu Africa
Christine Saidi, Kutztown University; Catherine Symone Fourshay, Susquehanna University; Rhonda M. Gonzalez, University of Texas at San Antonio

AFRICAN WORLD HISTORIES

Africanizing Democracies

1980–Present

Alicia C. Decker

Purdue University

Andrea L. Arrington

University of Arkansas

New York   Oxford
OXFORD UNIVERSITY PRESS

Oxford University Press is a department of the University of Oxford.
It furthers the University's objective of excellence in research,
scholarship, and education by publishing worldwide.

Oxford   New York
Auckland   Cape Town   Dar es Salaam   Hong Kong   Karachi
Kuala Lumpur   Madrid   Melbourne   Mexico City   Nairobi
New Delhi   Shanghai   Taipei   Toronto

With offices in
Argentina   Austria   Brazil   Chile   Czech Republic   France   Greece
Guatemala   Hungary   Italy   Japan   Poland   Portugal   Singapore
South Korea   Switzerland   Thailand   Turkey   Ukraine   Vietnam

For titles covered by Section 112 of the US Higher Education
Opportunity Act, please visit www.oup.com/us/he for the
latest information about pricing and alternate formats.

Published by Oxford University Press
198 Madison Avenue, New York, New York 10016
http://www.oup.com

Oxford is a registered trademark of Oxford University Press

Library of Congress Cataloging-in-Publication Data
Decker, Alicia Catharine, author.
  African world histories : Africanizing democracies, 1980–present /
Alicia Decker, Purdue University ; Andrea Arrington, University of Arkansas.
    pages cm
  ISBN 978-0-19-991539-2
  1. Democratization--Africa. 2. Africa--Politics and government--1960-
I. Arrington, Andrea, author. II. Title. III. Title: Africanizing democracies,
1980–present.
  JQ1879.A15D385 2014
  320.96--dc23
                                                        2013046082
Printing number: 9 8 7 6 5 4 3 2 1
Printed in the United States of America
on acid-free paper

ABOUT THE COVER -
Young Egyptian artists responded boldly to the political revolution sweeping through their coun-
try in 2011. Using walls in urban spaces as their canvases, artists showed their demands for
change by creating evocative murals and posters in support of the revolution. In this image, the
card being held up sends a message that Egyptian youth are paying attention to the political scene
and are not merely passive observers. This piece was photographed for the Walls of Freedom:
Street Art of the Egyptian Revolution *book project, edited by Basma Hamdy and Don Karl.*

CONTENTS

Maps and Figures

MAPS

FIGURES

Acknowledgments

We are grateful to Trevor Getz and Charles Cavaliere for providing us with the opportunity to contribute to this important series and for giving us the chance to work on our first collaborative project together. We are indebted to Jessica Ward for her extensive research, which allowed us to navigate the various topics presented throughout this text. The anonymous reviewers of the manuscript offered many useful critiques and suggestions that guided us through the revision process. We thank them for the time and careful consideration they gave to the project. Finally, we appreciate the undergraduate students we have taught over the years who have inspired many pedagogical discussions between the two of us about how to best serve the eclectic interests of our ever-curious student population. We hope this book is engaging to undergraduates and helps them understand more about contemporary Africa. We write this in honor of a dearly departed friend who gave unconditional support to Alicia's teaching, research, and writing.

Introduction: Africanizing Democracies or Democratizing Africa?

In 2007, Mo Ibrahim, a wealthy businessman born in Sudan, initiated the Mo Ibrahim Prize. The award is remarkable in that it is the largest individual prize given in the world. Recipients are awarded $5 million dollars over ten years and $200,000 per year thereafter for life.[1] The candidate pool is small and exclusive. The award is geared toward African heads of state who were democratically elected and fulfilled their mandated terms, who are within three years of leaving office, and who are thought to have demonstrated exceptional leadership. The selection committee looks for leaders who they believe helped alleviate poverty during their tenure and initiated sustainable and equitable development policies and projects. Ultimately, the prize is meant to highlight extraordinary leaders and models of good governance in a continent renowned for its dictators, corruption, and civil strife. It is not an easy prize to win, however; since its inception only three former African leaders have been awarded the prize. President Joaquim Alberto Chissano from Mozambique won the inaugural award in 2007, followed by President Festus Gontebanye Mogae of Botswana in 2008 and President Pedro de Verona Rodrigues Pires of Cape Verde in 2011.

The Mo Ibrahim Prize raises several important questions when considering the trajectory of Africa over the last three decades. Why must there be a prize for African leaders who fulfill what *should be* the mandate of every leader in every state of the world? Is there a standard of good governance that can be applied to every leader worldwide, or might good governance look different country by country? Implicit in the award criteria is the idea that good governance and just, forward-thinking leaders are what Africa desperately needs, yet the fact that the award was granted only three times in six years indicates that Africa is still far from achieving widespread and long-term

---

[1] All dollar amounts refer to U.S. currency or its equivalent.

good governance. Discourse in and out of Africa about how to "improve" the continent's political, economic, and social landscapes focus heavily on democratization. Discussions about politics, economic development, social welfare, human rights, environmental sustainability, natural resource exploitation, and public health are often connected to an overarching concern with democracy in African countries. This discourse implies that with democracy will come all the positive changes that so many Africans desire. But if democracy *is* the answer to so many of the major problems plaguing African countries, why has it not been more eagerly implemented? Why does the Mo Ibrahim Prize selection committee have such difficulty finding winners for the yearly award?

Observers of recent political change in Africa often talk of the "roadmap to democracy." To many inside and outside observers, it would seem that there is a way to map out the democratization process and that there is a standard framework or template for "democracy." Despite sustained pressure on African governments to democratize, most states are not considered "true" democracies and not all Africans believe democratization is the solution to many of the challenges they face in their daily lives and political systems. We are then left wondering if democracy is truly possible, or even desirable, in Africa. Is it possible to conceive of good governance without it being attached to democracy? Is democracy a one-size-fits-all endeavor, or could there be Africanized democracies that reflect the unique political, economic, and social cultures of each individual state? Is democracy antithetical to African values and beliefs? Are African leaders being misled by outsiders to believe that it is the only appropriate political system to implement? These are some of the major questions framing our examination of the past thirty years in Africa.

So what is democracy? Broadly speaking, if a group of people have the ability to choose and replace their leaders through regular, free, and fair elections, they have an *electoral democracy*. This says nothing about the actual quality of the political system, however, because competition "does not ensure high levels of freedom, quality, transparency, social justice, or other liberal values" (Diamond, 2008, p. 23). Electoral democracies make these values more achievable, but they do not ensure them. A *liberal democracy*, on the other hand, is one that is governed by the rule of law and that protects private property and civil liberties. The state also provides equality under the law, due process, checks and balances, protection of minorities, and freedom of expression. An open media and an active civil society are other important features. Some scholars suggest that the basic premises of liberalism, such as the importance of the individual, are not necessarily relevant to African cultures. Instead, alternative mechanisms of authority, such as ethnicity, patronage, and violence, may be more important (Moss, 2007).

We have deliberately titled this book *Africanizing Democracies* because we are interested in the ways in which Africans have constructed and reshaped democracy in order to fit their own political ideals and agendas. The late Tanzanian president Julius Nyerere described democracy in this way:

> Democracy means that the people must be able to choose freely those who govern them, and in broad terms determine what the government does in their name. It means that a government must be accountable to the people; it must also be responsive to views expressed freely through a political machinery that the people can understand and use. They will only understand and use it if that machinery makes sense in terms of their own culture, and is accessible with the framework of their own income and educational levels. (Nyerere, 2000, pp. xii–xiii)

Nyerere's definition has a decidedly liberal bent, although it is important to remember that he ruled Tanzania for twenty-one years as a semi-autocratic one-party state. Like most African leaders, his government fell somewhere along the autocracy–democracy spectrum. Indeed, there are democratically elected governments that do not protect civil liberties, just as there are some autocratic governments that do.

Democratization is a complex historical process by which a country moves away from authoritarian rule and toward a political system that is more democratic and participatory. "At the very least," argues South African political scientist Shireen Hassim, "any desirable form of democracy must encompass the civil and political rights advocated by liberalism, the socio-economic freedoms at the heart of socialism, and the cultural freedoms envisaged by feminism" (Hassim, 2006, p. 929). Democratization must enable the voices of the marginalized, particularly women, to be heard in formal institutions of the state and ensure that representation leads to greater equality for the vast majority of citizens. It should also "encompass the movement toward the recognition of women's sexual autonomy, bodily integrity, and rights to cultural self-definition" (Hassim, 2006, p. 931). In other words, democratization is about creating a space for the inclusion of larger numbers of voices and interests, both within and beyond the realm of formal politics. In the following chapters we explore the extent to which political democratization has opened up, or democratized, other political arenas.

This book analyzes democratization in Africa, a vast continent that is home to fifty-five sovereign countries. This includes the Sahrawi Arab Democratic Republic, or Western Sahara, which is a heavily contested territory in North Africa. It is recognized as a sovereign member of the African Union (AU), although the Moroccan government also claims it as a territory. Because of this dispute, Morocco is the only African country that is not a member of the AU. Another contested territory is the Republic of Somaliland, which is an autonomous region of Somalia. Because it is not yet recognized by the international community, Somaliland is not usually considered an African "country," unlike Western Sahara. Although we have attempted to cover as much of the continent as possible, we have focused most of our attention on fully sovereign nations and their experiences with democratization since 1980. Whenever necessary, we have differentiated between North Africa and sub-Saharan Africa.

As much as possible, we have tried to privilege the voices of Africans from all walks of life, not just the "big men" who tend to be referenced in most discussions about formal politics and certainly not just the perspectives of outsiders who insert themselves into discourse on democracy in Africa. On the other hand, it is of course important to include the actions and ideologies expressed by those in positions of power, whether they be African politicians or non-African leaders and advisers, because they heavily influence the ways that Africans themselves view the political, economic, and social landscapes of their own countries. In an effort to find a balance between "high" and "low" politics, we have utilized a wide variety of primary sources from numerous social actors (e.g., newspaper articles, speeches, memoirs, films, letters, photographs, and even conversational anecdotes based on our own fieldwork experiences). We have also tried to use as much African scholarship as possible, although we recognize that many important voices (and case studies) are still missing because of spatial constraints. At the end of each chapter you will find suggested readings, films, and websites that provide some additional African perspectives.

Each chapter in this volume focuses on a different aspect of democratization in Africa. We believe that political democratization, whether in theory or in practice, has had a significant impact on the continent's economic, social, and cultural landscape. This, in turn, has created new opportunities and challenges for ordinary Africans. At the same time, African realities have also helped to shape broader discussions about democratization. In the following chapters, we explore the ways in which political democratization has influenced, and has been influenced by, developments in various economic, social, and cultural spheres. Chapter 1 deals explicitly with political developments and includes discussions of the Greenbelt Movement, the end of apartheid, the role of women in politics, and the Arab Spring. Chapter 2 focuses on economic activities and realities, with case studies on Structural Adjustment Programs, debt relief and humanitarian aid, resource wars, and the explosive boom of Chinese investment and aid in Africa. Chapter 3 examines health and healing challenges in the wake of democratization, with specific consideration of HIV/AIDS, malaria and tuberculosis, maternal mortality, and mental illness. In Chapter 4 we turn our attention toward movements for women, gender, and sexuality rights, with an examination of academic feminism, the Maputo Protocol, female genital cutting, and gay rights. Finally, Chapter 5 explores major security challenges in modern Africa with case studies on corruption, famine and food insecurity, sexual and gender-based violence, and peacemaking, peacekeeping, and peacebuilding.

REFERENCES

Diamond, Larry. *The Spirit of Democracy: The Struggle to Build Free Societies throughout the World*. New York: Henry Holt and Company, 2008.

Hassim, Shireen. "Democratization: A View from Africa." *Signs: Journal of Women in Culture and Society* 31, no. 4 (2006): 928–932.

Moss, Todd. *African Development: Making Sense of the Issues and Actors*. Boulder, Colo.: Lynne Rienner, 2007.

Nyerere, Julius K. "Forward." In *What Is Africa's Problem?*, by Yoweri K. Museveni. Minneapolis: University of Minnesota Press, 2000.

SUGGESTED READINGS/FILMS/WEBSITES

Bates, Robert H. *When Things Fell Apart: State-Failure in Late-Century Africa*. Cambridge, U.K.: Cambridge University Press, 2008.

Cooper, Frederick. *Africa since 1940: The Past of the Present*. Cambridge, U.K.: Cambridge University Press, 2002.

Nugent, Paul. *Africa since Independence*. 2d ed. London: Palgrave Macmillan, 2012.

Radelet, Steven. *Emerging Africa: How 17 Countries Are Leading the Way*. Washington, D.C.: Center for Global Development, 2010.

Politics

Political democratization in Africa is not a recent phenomenon but instead can be traced back to the constitutional changes implemented by interim governments in the late 1950s and early 1960s in order to facilitate decolonization. After independence, however, most support for democratic governance ceased. African leaders were more concerned with rapid development and liberating the economy from neocolonial control. They thought that political pluralism was "a luxury that poor countries could not afford" because it would divert attention away from the problems of underdevelopment (Young, 1996, pp. 54–55). Many leaders therefore adopted a Soviet-style approach that emphasized central planning and state-led development. By concentrating political authority in the hands of a few rather than dispersing it more broadly through democratic institutions, newly independent states thought that they could develop more efficiently.

The second wave of political democratization was much more subtle and took place in the late 1970s and early 1980s as military dictatorships and one-party states began falling apart. In 1979 alone, three of the continent's most notorious dictators were overthrown (Idi Amin of Uganda, Jean-Bédel Bokassa of the Central African Republic, and Francisco Macias Nguema of Equatorial Guinea). Some single-party states attempted to amass political legitimacy by allowing parliamentary elections within the ruling party. These elections provided the public with a space in which to voice their discontent, even if they did not produce any substantive political changes. Nigeria and Ghana both experienced important, albeit temporary, political openings in 1979. Apart from these two cases, most political openings of this wave were part of a liberalized autocracy and did not represent fully democratic regimes.

The most recent wave of democratization was a product of global politics and local dissent. With the collapse of the Berlin Wall and the end of the Cold War in 1989, African governments found that they were no longer able to count on the United States or the Soviet Union for external support. If they wanted to continue receiving donor funds, they had to agree to a number of explicit conditions, namely democratization and respect for human rights. At the same time, citizens began challenging authorities on corruption and agitating for greater political freedoms. In Benin, for instance, the country was mired in political and economic crisis by early 1990. The central bank had collapsed, civil servant and student strikes were rampant, and daily life was nearly impossible. Government efforts to quell dissent resulted in even larger protests. President Mathew Kérékou, who had ruled the country as a Marxist one-party state for sixteen years, had become desperate and agreed to hold a National Conference of Active Forces of the Nation. Convened in February 1990, the conference included representatives from opposition parties, civil liberties organizations, professional bodies, and religious groups. After attendees took the bold step of declaring themselves the governing body of the nation, Kérékou agreed to step down. When elections were held in March of the following year, the president was defeated by the interim prime minister. The National Conference and the peaceful transition to multiparty democracy were unprecedented, and within three years eleven other countries had followed suit. Some resulted in political transitions (Niger and Mali), while others did not (Togo). But by the mid-1990s, nearly all African countries had held some type of multiparty elections.

President Olesegun Obasanjo was one of the central figures in the third wave of political democratization. He led the Nigerian government for three years after the military ruler, General Murtala Mohammed, was assassinated in an abortive coup in 1976. Once civilian rule was re-established in 1979, Obasanjo stepped down from power. Although he was a military man, he was also a strong proponent of democratization. He argued that democracy was the "best and most humane form of power" but insisted that it must take a distinctly African form (Obasanjo, 1992, p. 59). He maintained that the pursuit of justice was essential to the democratic process, as were the following "essential and vital ingredients":

1. Trust creation and confidence building between the leaders and the populace
2. Periodic elections of political leadership through the secret ballot
3. Creation of an appropriate political machinery
4. Promotion and defense of human rights
5. Political communication
6. Decentralization of political power and authority
7. Education and political education

Obasanjo firmly believed that political authority must be institutionalized instead of taking on a patrimonial character. He insisted that "[t]hose who govern must not behave as if authority or power is their personal property and something they can hand down to their heirs." Instead, they should "acknowledge that they are only representatives of the nation and not the owners or proprietors of sovereignty" (Obasanjo, 1992, p. 62).

In an effort to improve the capacity and competence of African leaders, Obasanjo created the African Leadership Forum, which met four times between November 1990 and May 1991. The last meeting was held in Kampala and was attended by five current heads of state, three former heads of state, diplomats, scholars, business leaders, and representatives of student and women's organizations. Attendees debated four key issues: security, stability, development, and cooperation. Out of this process came a statement of principles, which became known as the Kampala Document (Deng and Zartman, 2002). The Document addressed the problem of security and stability in Africa and confirmed that democratization was a prerequisite for cooperation and development. Participants in the conference believed that Africa needed a new policy framework with which to engage the international community. The framework may have been too ambitious and threatening to African governments, since it went dormant after Obasanjo was imprisoned by Sani Abacha, Nigeria's then military head of state. After Obasanjo was released from prison following Abacha's death in June 1998 and then elected president in February

1999, he revived the movement. Shortly thereafter, the Organization of African Unity (OAU) adopted the Kampala Document as a reflection of their values and promised to monitor its implementation.

The fact that the African Leadership Forum went completely dormant after its founder was imprisoned says a great deal about the challenges that accompany political democratization in Africa. It reflects a contradictory political trend that Larry Diamond identifies as democratic progress and retreat. On the one hand, there are more electoral democracies in Africa today than ever before. Between 1980 and 2007, the number of democracies on the continent doubled, while the number of authoritarian states decreased from approximately one-half to one-third (Tripp et al., 2009, p. 8). On the other hand, many of these democracies are poor in quality and can be easily reversed. In January 2012, for instance, a massive insurgency tore through northern Mali, fueled in large part by the influx of heavy weaponry following the 2011 civil war in Libya. When government forces were unable to quell the rebellion, a faction of the military staged a coup d'état and ousted the democratically elected president from power. Islamists used this as an opportunity to seize control of the north from the rebels and implement Islamic law (*sharia* law). The violent crisis came to an end in January 2013 when French armed forces intervened and recaptured the embattled northern region. Six months later elections were held and some semblance of "democracy" was restored to Mali. Although this is perhaps an extreme case, significant democratic backsliding can also be seen in Togo, Gabon, Guinea, and Uganda with the repeal of constitutional term limits. Other serious problems include a lack of adherence to the rule of law, infringements on freedoms of expression and association, widespread corruption, and discrimination against women and members of the lesbian, gay, bisexual, transgender, and queer communities.

Freedom House, a nongovernmental organization that conducts research and advocacy on issues related to democracy, political freedom, and human rights, conducts an annual survey that evaluates the state of global freedom as experienced by individuals. Freedom is measured according to the enjoyment of political rights and civil liberties. A country that is labeled "free" is one where there is open political competition, a climate of respect for civil liberties, significant independent civic life, and an autonomous media. One that is "partly free" has limited respect for political rights and civil liberties. Finally, in a country that is "not free," basic political rights are absent and civil liberties are widely and systematically denied. According to the most recent *Freedom in the World Report*, 22 percent of countries in sub-Saharan Africa (SSA) were free, 37 percent were partly free, and 41 percent were not free (Freedom House, 2013). When broken down by population, 13 percent of the population in SSA was free, 51 percent was partly free, and 36 percent was not free. Ghana was the country with the highest rating, meaning that its citizens enjoyed the most political rights and civil liberties, while Sudan, Eritrea, and Somalia had the lowest ratings. The Freedom House website describes their rating system in detail and provides historical data for each country, which makes it a highly useful tool for tracking democratization in Africa across time.

The African Peer Review Mechanism (APRM) performs a similar function by monitoring African countries' progress in four key areas: democracy and political governance, economic governance and management, corporate governance, and socioeconomic development. In March 2003, the African Union (AU) established this voluntary program under the auspices of the New Partnership for Africa's Development (NEPAD) in order to encourage participating nations to conform to a number of collectively agreed upon governance standards. Participants promise to complete periodic self-assessments that evaluate their compliance with a range of African and international human rights treaties and standards. As of early 2012, thirty-three countries had formally joined the program. The APRM reflects the African Union's professed commitment to democratization as enshrined under Articles 3 and 4 of their organizational charter. It is the key mechanism that promotes adherence to and fulfillment of the commitments made in the NEPAD Declaration on Democracy, Political, Economic, and Corporate Governance, which was adopted in June 2002 at the AU Summit in Durban and the African Charter on Democracy, Governance, and Elections, adopted in January 2007 at the AU Summit in Addis Ababa. The latter entered into force as part of international law on February 15, 2012.

Throughout the remainder of this chapter, we examine four distinct case studies that demonstrate the various ways in which political democratization has taken shape on the continent. The first explores the evolution of the Green Belt Movement in Kenya, which began as a small tree-planting campaign and quickly grew into one of the world's largest and most successful pro-democracy movements. The second considers the end of apartheid and the emergence of multiparty politics as watersheds in the history of political democratization in Africa. In the third section we consider the significant rise of women in politics over the last three decades and what this trend says about the status of democracy in Africa today. The final case study reflects upon the Arab Spring and what this movement means (or could mean) for democratization in North Africa.

THE GREEN BELT MOVEMENT

Political democratization in Africa has been inextricably linked to other struggles for social, economic, and environmental justice. Nowhere is this more apparent than in Kenya, where a small tree-planting campaign gradually developed into one of the most vibrant and successful pro-democracy movements the world has ever seen. In 1977, Wangari Maathai established the Green Belt Movement under the auspices of the National Council of Women of Kenya in order to address the major environmental concerns that were threatening rural women's health and livelihoods. Maathai encouraged women to work together to grow seedlings and to plant trees so as to create a number of ecologically rich "green belts" throughout the country. She soon realized that environmental degradation, deforestation, and food insecurity were the result of community disempowerment. Because the poor did not understand that they had the power to change their political, economic, and environmental circumstances, she began offering seminars in civic and environmental education. Through these workshops, participants learned to advocate for greater democratic space and to demand more accountability from their leaders.

The Green Belt Movement gradually became increasingly politicized. In October 1989, President Daniel Arap Moi announced that he would be taking over Uhuru Park, the only remaining park in the capital city of Nairobi, to construct a sixty-two-story building, the highest in Africa. He planned to erect a four-story statue of himself directly adjacent to the high-rise. Not only would this "development" destroy valuable green space, but it would also increase the nation's already substantial external debt. Maathai and a small group of Movement participants staged a protest in the park and were subsequently beaten by the police. She later took the matter to court, arguing that the park belonged to the people and therefore could not be privatized. Although the judge disagreed and sided with the president, the Movement emerged victorious when financial backers decided to withdraw their support because of the tremendous public outcry. Members of

Parliament were outraged, chastising them as "a bunch of divorcées and irresponsible women," and recommended that they be banned for subversion (Maathai, 2000, p. 38).

Several years later, in March 1992, Maathai returned to the park with a small group of women whose sons had been detained for demanding democratic rights and mounted a hunger strike in a place they dubbed Freedom Corner. After peacefully occupying the park for five days, the government called in the police to break up the gathering. Maathai and three others were brutally beaten and taken to the hospital. The international community was outraged, but the president refused to release the political prisoners. The women would not give up and moved their protest across the street to All Saint's Cathedral, where they remained for the next year. Although the government harassed the women and tried to intimidate them into leaving, they were steadfast and refused to leave until their sons were eventually released in early 1993.

During the summer of 1998, Maathai learned that the Kenyan government was planning to privatize large areas of public land in the Karura Forest, an area just outside Nairobi, and give it to political supporters. In addition to writing numerous letters of protest, she gathered a group of Movement supporters and went to the forest to plant trees. In early January 1999, she returned to the forest with her colleagues. This time, their entry was blocked by a large number of men. When she attempted to plant a tree in an area that was going to be cleared for a golf course, the guards attacked the group. Maathai and many others were injured, but the police refused to arrest the assailants. The event provoked international outrage, and riots broke out in Nairobi. Unrest continued to haunt the capital until August 16, 1999, when the president announced that he was banning the allocation of all public land. In other words, Maathai and her Green Belt Movement had won again.

In October 2004, Maathai was awarded the Nobel Peace Prize for her contribution to sustainable development, democracy, and peace. She was the first African woman and the first environmentalist to win the prize. In her acceptance speech, Maathai explained why tree-planting was linked to political democratization and peace:

> Although initially the Green Belt Movement's tree planting activities did not address issues of democracy and peace, it soon became clear that responsible governance of the environment was impossible without democratic space. Therefore, the tree became a symbol for the democratic struggle in Kenya. Citizens were mobilized

to challenge widespread abuses of power, corruption and environmental misman-
agement. In Nairobi's Uhuru Park, at Freedom Corner, and in many parts of the
country, trees of peace were planted to demand the release of prisoners of con-
science and a peaceful transition to democracy. Through the Green Belt Movement, thousands of ordinary citizens were mobilized and empowered to take action
and effect change. They learned to overcome fear and a sense of helplessness and
moved to defend democratic rights. (Maathai, 2004)

Kenyans were ultimately victorious. In December 2002, they voted to
oust the ruling party from power, thus ending nearly forty years of
authoritarian rule. Their politicization was due, in no small part, to the
courageous efforts of Maathai and her Green Belt Movement. Sadly,
Maathai died from complications of ovarian cancer on September 25,
2011, at the age of 71. Her legacy lives on through the Green Belt
Movement, which to date has planted over 51 million trees while empowering women and girls, fostering democratic space, and promoting sustainable livelihoods.

THE END OF APARTHEID

On May 10, 1994, the world watched as Nelson Mandela was inaugurated as the first black president of South Africa. President Mandela,
a former political dissenter who spent twenty-seven years in jail for
his open critique of and challenge to the apartheid state, was a beloved figure within South Africa and earned the respect of outsiders
for his stoic commitment to democracy. This inaugural moment was
hailed as a crucial element in the democratization of the African continent, and there was high expectation that under Mandela's tenure,
South Africa would become an example of good governance for other
African states to follow.

That the end of apartheid did not come until so late in the twentieth
century is testament to the strength of this segregationist policy
and the determination by the white minority in South Africa to maintain political, economic, and social hegemony. When the Afrikaner-
supported National Party gained power in 1948, the new government
was quick to implement the system of apartheid promised in its election campaign. Apartheid, or "separateness" in Afrikaans, was designed
to limit the political and economic activities of the African majority in
order to minimize their power in South African society while securing
the position of the white minority. Apartheid was also used to separate

and often isolate races and ethnic groups to limit interactions between different populations. South African sociologist Deborah Posel describes apartheid as a system that

> offered the promise of heightened discipline, regulation and surveillance: boundaries were to be reasserted and spaces reorganised, the movements of people systematised and contained, races rescued from 'impurity', the notion of family rehabilitated and 'the savage discipline of tribal life' restored. . . . Apartheid's principal imagery was of a society in which every 'race' knew and observed its proper place—economically, politically, and socially. Race was to be the critical and over-riding faultline. . . . (Posel, 2001, p. 52)

Many significant apartheid laws were passed in the 1950s at a time when the rest of sub-Saharan Africa was beginning to plan for decolonization and democratization. Black South Africans continued to live under the oppressive apartheid system throughout the 1980s when the gradual repeal of apartheid legislation occurred. From the early days of the imposition of apartheid legislation, black and mixed-race Africans fought hard against the racist white minority government. Mandela, as part of the African National Congress (ANC), spearheaded a civil disobedience movement in protest of the laws requiring that the entire population be racially classified and then segregated. Other organizations, such as the Pan Africanist Congress of Azania (PAC), the South African Communist Party (SACP), and the African Resistance Movement (ARM), also worked tirelessly against apartheid.

In response to the brutal Sharpeville Massacre of 1960 and the government's subsequent declaration of a state of emergency, organized protests by political organizations moved away from their traditional stance of nonviolence toward a more militant ideology, thus marking a new era in the anti-apartheid movement. Mandela's leadership in the militant wing of the ANC resulted in his arrest and sentencing of life imprisonment. Numerous members of other anti-apartheid groups were also targeted and punished by the South African government. By the late 1970s, the country was in a constant state of protest and violence as its black population and other opponents of apartheid fought for democracy in the form of majority rule. During the 1980s, protests and riots were so commonplace in African townships (urban settlement areas reserved for nonwhite populations) that the government was forced to declare another state of emergency, which lasted from 1984 until 1989.

In 1989, F. W. de Klerk was elected president of South Africa. Although he was a member of the National Party, de Klerk focused on dismantling the apartheid state while establishing a new constitution based on the democratic concept of "one person, one vote." He dissolved the legislation that was used to justify Mandela's imprisonment and in 1990 ordered his release. Mandela then worked with de Klerk on the country's democratic transition. By 1991, all apartheid laws were repealed and plans were laid for a multiparty election to be held in 1994.

President Mandela's inauguration speech reflected a conciliatory approach to moving forward after the end of white minority rule. He stated:

> Today, all of us . . . confer glory and hope to newborn liberty. Out of the experience of an extraordinary human disaster that lasted too long, must be born a society of which all humanity will be proud. . . . The time for the healing of the wounds has come. The moment to bridge that [sic] chasms that divide us has come. . . . We have, at last, achieved our political emancipation. . . . We commit ourselves to the construction of a complete, just and lasting peace. . . . We must therefore act together as a united people, for national reconciliation, for nation building, for the birth of a new world. (Mandela, 1994)

Mandela and the new government took seriously the concept of reconciliation. In 1995, the government passed the Promotion of National Unity and Reconciliation Act, which formed the framework for the Truth and Reconciliation Commission (TRC). Under the leadership of Archbishop Desmond Tutu, the TRC was tasked with investigating human rights abuses during the period of 1960 to 1994, providing support for victims that would allow for compensation and rehabilitation and considering applications for amnesty of perpetrators of human rights violations. The TRC was meant to provide closure and aid in the development of a shared national identity in order to preserve the fledgling democracy while allowing the country to improve its economic and social conditions.

The end of apartheid and Nelson Mandela's stewardship of African democracy marks an important feature of the continent's history. President Mandela's leadership was built on the ideology of good governance and solid state-building. Mandela decided not to run for re-election, despite being the clear favorite, because he felt he had served his purpose in setting the groundwork for democracy. His decision to step down voluntarily also sent a strong message to other African leaders—many of whom by the late 1990s had been in power for over a decade—that for democracy to succeed, term limits and free and fair elections were necessities. Although this message may not have been taken to heart by Africa's long-reigning leaders, the continental popularity of the beloved statesman speaks to the respect earned by Mandela and the desire by Africans for more leaders like him.

WOMEN AND POLITICAL PARTICIPATION

One of the most exciting developments to accompany recent democratization efforts in Africa is the substantial increase in women's political participation.[1] According to a UN women's biennial report, *Progress of the World's Women: In Pursuit of Justice*, women held an average of 20 percent of the ministerial positions in sub-Saharan Africa in 2010 (UN Women, 2011). In North Africa they held 5 percent. Cape Verde had the highest level of representation at 53 percent, while Libya and the Comoros had the lowest at zero. As of April 2013, women in sub-Saharan Africa held 21 percent of parliamentary seats, a significant jump from the average of 9 percent in 1997. Those in North Africa held nearly 19 percent of seats (versus only 2.6 percent in 1997). Rwanda currently has the highest percentage of women parliamentarians at 56 percent, while Egypt has the lowest at 2 percent. Today, women hold more than 40 percent of parliamentary seats in the Seychelles, Senegal, and South Africa and more than 35 percent of seats in Mozambique, Tanzania, and Uganda. They also serve as speakers of the house in eight African countries: Botswana, Gabon, Mozambique, Rwanda, Swaziland, Tanzania, Uganda, and Zimbabwe. Since the mid-1980s, three women have served as unelected heads of state. Carmen Pereira was appointed as Guinea Bissau's acting head of state for three days in 1984, Ruth Perry served as chair of the six-member collective presidency in Liberia from 1996 to 1997, and, most recently, Joyce Banda assumed the presidency of Malawi in April 2012. Ellen Johnson Sirleaf of Liberia continues to serve as Africa's first elected female president, a position she has held since 2006.

---

[1] It is important to note that African women have always participated in politics and various forms of political action. These "traditional" structures remain important and often run parallel to Western-style political systems.

This promising trend raises a host of interesting questions about women's leadership and whether a female politician is more likely to be democratic or woman-friendly than a man. Most African women have gotten involved in politics as a result of quota systems. This is an important development because as Shireen Hassim argues, "Without representation in legislatures, women citizens have a diminished ability to hold governments accountable." The South African political scientist maintains that, "There can also be little doubt that better functioning and more effective state institutions are in the interest of poor women, and the extent to which women become part of electoral and policy constituencies is an important marker of the democratic nature of the state" (Hassim, 2006, p. 930). Yet women's participation in politics is not enough. In order to advance democratization and gender equality, women (and men) must instill feminist content into their policymaking.

FIGURE 1.1   Ellen Johnson Sirleaf is sworn in as Liberia's president at the Capitol Building in Monrovia, Liberia on January 16, 2006. In this momentous ceremony, attended by dignitaries from around the world, she was inaugurated as Africa's first elected female president. Photograph by Charles Dharapak of the Associated Press.

They must ensure that the voices of the marginalized are heard within the formal institutions of the state and that their representation leads to greater equality for the vast majority of women and men.

Ellen Johnson Sirleaf is one politician who has strived to do this very thing. When she was inaugurated as Africa's first elected female president on January 16, 2006, she faced enormous challenges. Liberia had just emerged from fourteen years of brutal civil war and had very little in the way of infrastructure. The country had been riddled by corruption and was saddled with an enormous debt burden. In her first address to the nation, the "Iron Lady," so dubbed because of her iron will and steely determination, ardently vowed to turn things around:

> We pledge anew our commitment to transparency, open government, and participatory democracy for all of our citizens. . . . Committed to advance the spirit of inclusion, I assure all Liberians and our international partners and friends that our Government will recognize and support a strong democratic and loyal opposition in Liberia. This is important because we believe that our democratic culture and our nation are best served when the opposition is strong and actively engaged in the process of nation building. . . . My Administration therefore commits itself to the creation of a democracy in which the constitutional and civil liberties and rights of all of our people will be respected. (Sirleaf, 2006)

Sirleaf's efforts to transform the political culture of the nation are highlighted in the powerful documentary, *Iron Ladies of Liberia* (Junge and Johnson, 2007), which chronicles her first year in office. Throughout the film, viewers get a good sense of what it actually takes to rebuild a tattered country after years of civil war. Although Sirleaf accomplished a great deal during her first term in office, including stabilizing the economy, bringing water and electricity to most of the capital, and launching a free primary school education program, political opponents were outraged by her decision to run for re-election. When she was one of three persons awarded the Nobel Peace Prize on October 7, 2011, just four days prior to the election, rivals said that she did not deserve the award because of her ties to the former rebel leader–president Charles Taylor. Members of the opposition criticized the international community for giving her an unfair advantage. Despite these cries of foul play, Sirleaf won the election by a landslide and was inaugurated for a second term on January 16, 2012. Whether she will be able to continue moving the country toward greater democratization remains to be seen. What her electoral victory suggests, however, is that most Liberians believe that a woman remains the best candidate for the job.

THE ARAB SPRING

In December 2010, a policewoman reportedly slapped and spit on a young man living in Sidi Bouzid, a rural town in Tunisia, after he refused to relinquish his fruit and vegetable cart and scales. After the altercation, the man—Mohammed Bouazizi—attempted to meet with municipality administrators to complain about his treatment by the policewoman, but they would not speak with him. In response, Bouazizi returned to the provincial headquarters, doused himself in a flammable liquid, and set himself on fire. He died from his injuries two and a half weeks later, but his self-immolation set off a series of revolutions throughout North Africa and the Middle East. The complaints voiced by Tunisians in late 2010 resonated strongly with Egyptians and Libyans, who also formed revolutionary movements to push out long-reigning dictators in hopes of democratization. The Arab Spring, as it came to be known, effected change in three African countries and throughout parts of the Middle East as the revolutionaries demanded democracy, increased job opportunities, and improved economic conditions.

Tunisians interpreted Bouazizi's extreme act as a protest against a government and police force unconcerned with the lives of average, impoverished citizens. President Zine el Abidine Ben Ali came to power in 1987 when he organized a bloodless coup while serving as prime minister. By 2010, when Bouazizi set himself on fire, Ben Ali had been in power for twenty-three years. Ben Ali escaped widespread criticism of his emerging dictatorship in the 1990s as his regime helped stabilize the country in other ways. His government welcomed not only funding but also advice from the World Bank and the Islamic Development Bank in the 1990s, and Tunisia's economy recorded strong growth and economic diversification while avoiding inflation (Hassan, 2005). This set Ben Ali's leadership apart from his predecessor in the 1980s and gained him widespread support among Tunisians. Ben Ali's government also took progressive steps forward in terms of women's rights. As sociologist Mounira M. Charrad explains, a second major wave of reforms that helped women gain higher status in Tunisian society and in the legal system occurred in the 1990s, spearheaded by a 1993 provision that established the descent of nationality to be through Tunisian women, not men. This legislation was "an important step toward allowing women to become equal citizens in the nation-state," and Ben Ali's administration was regaled as progressive and pro-women because of this reform (Charrad, 2007, p. 1524).

Although there were some positive aspects to Tunisia's trajectory in the 1990s, there were also signs that he was not fulfilling his promise to implement gradual democratization. After seizing power in 1987, Ben Ali proceeded to "win" elections in 1989 and 1994 as the sole candidate. Even with the introduction of multiparty politics in 1999, he easily won re-election. This was not the democratization that Tunisians hoped for, and instead, they witnessed amendments to the constitution that allowed Ben Ali to serve additional terms. Even as the World Bank, the Islamic Development Bank, and Ben Ali's administration congratulated themselves for positive economic growth in the 1990s, there were also warnings from Bank advisers that Tunisia had to address the growing unemployment rate of its relatively well-educated citizens. By the time Bouazizi demonstrated his frustration with the government through self-immolation, countless other Tunisians were experiencing the same disillusionment with Ben Ali's regime, and they quickly responded by organizing protests. The president responded to the growing outrage by visiting Bouazizi in the hospital, but the gesture was an empty one as Tunisians pushed for democracy and change in their country. He tried to appease his angry country by dissolving his government and pushing up a parliamentary election by six months. It was too little, too late, however, and by the time Ben Ali declared Tunisia to be in a state of emergency, he had lost the loyalty of his military and police force. On January 14, 2011, Ben Ali fled the country, ending his twenty-three-year reign.

The revolution in Tunisia was only the start of protests to sweep through other Arab countries in North Africa and the Middle East. The energy behind the removal of Ben Ali was contagious as Egyptians and Libyans considered their country's own challenges and heavy-handed regimes. Several factors contributed to growing unrest and the vulnerability of the leaders in those countries, such as "years in power of the incumbent; size of the youth population cohort; democracy, corruption, press freedom, and GDP per capita (as a summary measure of economic performance)," but perhaps most problematic of all was disgust with "education and its connection with the economic environment" (Campante and Chor, 2012, pp. 167–168). Indeed, Tunisia, Egypt, and Libya had in common a relatively well-educated but under- or unemployed population. By the time of Bouazizi's self-immolation,

FIGURE 1.2   Throughout Cairo, young Egyptian artists created art in public spaces to visually represent their complaints against the Mubarak regime and the status quo. This mural is titled "Peace Machine" and was photographed in February 2012 for the *Walls of Freedom: Street Art of the Egyptian Revolution* book project, edited by Basma Hamdy and Don Karl.

Egyptians and Libyans were frustrated with the status quo of their countries and, inspired by the Tunisian revolution, began movements to overthrow their own regimes.

Egypt followed Tunisia's example, starting on January 25, 2011, with widespread protests that turned violent when thousands of Egyptians converged in Tahrir Square in Cairo. Police employed water cannons and tear gas to control the crowd, further instigating conflict in the square and throughout the country. As tensions escalated and more violence erupted, President Hosni Mubarak dissolved his cabinet but announced that he would not step down and ordered a curfew to be enforced by the military. On February 1, Mubarak declared that he would not seek re-election but that he was still unwilling to vacate the presidency. His refusal to leave pushed the country deeper into revolution, and on February 11, Mubarak officially resigned after holding his position for three decades. The military then assumed power, after which they dissolved the parliament and suspended the constitution. Violent protests continued until democratic presidential elections were held in June 2012. Muhamed Morsi, an Islamist politician allied with the Muslim Brotherhood, emerged victorious. After just one year in power, he too, was ousted by a military coup in July 2013.

The military named Adly Mansour, the head of the Supreme Constitutional Court, as interim president. However, the issue of leadership remains largely unresolved as supporters of the Muslim Brotherhood continue to protest Morsi's ouster. A constitutional referendum is expected to be held in January 2014, followed by a presidential election several months later. Libya's revolution started in February 2011 and ended in late October 2011 with the death of President Muammar Gaddafi, who had been in power since 1969, and the declaration by the National Transitional Council that Libya was fully liberated. Unlike other countries involved in this series of revolutions, Libya's ouster of Gaddafi involved external support, with military intervention from other Arab governments and NATO forces. Gaddafi's forty-two-year reign was marked by strong disassociation with the West and a focus on pan-Arab relations, though by the early 2000s Gaddafi had shown some interest in improving Libya's relationships with the rest of the world. By the time the Arab Spring moved into Libya, Gaddafi had become the target of protesters and human rights activists. Gaddafi was forced into hiding for eight months, during which he continued to lead government forces against rebel and NATO military strikes. The rebels set up an interim government in direct opposition to Gaddafi and gained support from numerous outside governments, such as the United States, the United Kingdom, and France. As the rebels gained momentum, they seized control over an increasing number of cities, including Sirte, where Gaddafi was found and killed on October 20, 2011. In July 2012, the National Transitional Council held the country's first democratic elections in more than four decades. Although some semblance of peace has returned to Libya, the country continues to experience significant political, economic, and social challenges.

As these three North African nations experience postrevolution growing pains, there are more questions than answers about how this phase will unfold. Perhaps the questions most often asked are if these countries will democratize and what "true democracy" entails. Many of the countries that underwent regime change during the Arab Spring are now governed by Islamists, leading some to wonder whether democratization will occur or if the Arab Spring instead paved the way for Islamist autocracies to obtain power. The fact that insiders and outsiders alike are questioning the authenticity of these democratizing states indicates that some of the other concerns cited as the most significant causes of the Arab Spring, such as the mismatching of educational background and job opportunities, may not be addressed or remedied by the new regimes. Interviews with residents of Sidi Bouzid, the Tunisian town where the Arab Spring originated, revealed that a year after the dismantling of Ben Ali's regime, Tunisians were still frustrated and waiting to see real change in their economic lives. In addition to continued high unemployment, there was concern that the new government had done little to communicate with the citizenry, and it was unclear how the new leadership planned to address the problems that sparked the revolution.

CONCLUSION

The year 1994 was important in contemporary Africa. While apartheid was coming to a close in South Africa, Rwanda was experiencing a genocide that left over 800,000 dead. Africa was showcasing two extreme versions of life on the continent. The end of apartheid and the democratic process that followed was hailed as a hallmark achievement and a model for the rest of the continent to follow, while the ethnic killing in Rwanda highlighted the fragility of security in modern African states. It was easy in 1994 to see South Africa as the shining star of Africa and Rwanda as the tragic example of Africa's failure to promote peace and stability. Interestingly though, within just ten to fifteen years there has been a reversal in the outside perceptions of these two countries. Since the genocide, Rwanda has been credited with fostering reconciliation as well as economic and political progress, thus becoming a darling of nongovernmental organizations that are eager to help rebuild a country shaken by violence and trauma. South Africa, on the other hand, concerns many interested observers because of lackluster governance following Nelson Mandela's time in office. Public health debacles, lack of initiative in resolving regional crises, and growing disillusionment with postapartheid policies and practices leave many wondering if South Africa is going to be one of Africa's next trouble spots.

    Indeed, in 2008, almost fifteen years after the end of apartheid, we asked a South African bus driver how life was going for him in the "new South Africa." He replied, "If you knew what life was like in the old South Africa, you know our life now." The promise and enthusiasm for all that a postapartheid South Africa would entail was still not a reality at least for some. There is no denying that major changes *did* sweep through that country, but the challenge as always is for the government to meet the needs and desires of as many of its citizens as it can, a daunting challenge that contemporary governments across the continent struggle to overcome. We need to question what conditions or "roadmaps" can really promote democratization in Africa and whether or not democratization guarantees progress as defined by Africans themselves. On the one hand, in countries like South Africa where much enthusiasm and respect was given to Nelson Mandela for his leadership, successors have failed to meet the standards set by previous leaders, which forces citizens and outsiders to question how stable democracy really is in Africa, or perhaps more significantly, what the limitations of democracy may be. Other countries, however, such as Rwanda, have seen periods of renewed hope in democratization and the ability of elected officials to help lead their countries out of a tragedy and into better days. Out of genocide come slivers of hope, just as out of an anti-apartheid struggle come signs of trouble ahead.

REFERENCES

Campante, Filipe R., and Davin Chor. "Why Was the Arab World Poised for Revolution? Schooling, Economic Opportunities, and the Arab Spring." *The Journal of Economic Perspectives* 26, no. 2 (Spring 2012): 167–188.

Charrad, Mounira M. "Tunisia at the Forefront of the Arab World: Two Waves of Gender Legislation." *Washington & Lee Law Review* 64 (2007): 1513–1527.

Deng, Francis M., and I. William Zartman. *A Strategic Vision for Africa: The Kampala Movement.* Washington, D.C.: The Brookings Institution, 2002.

Diamond, Larry. "The Rule of Law versus the Big Man." In *Democratization in Africa: Progress and Retreat*, 2d ed., edited by Larry Diamond and Marc F. Plattner, pp. 47–59. Baltimore: Johns Hopkins University Press, 2010.

Freedom House. *Freedom in the World Report.* Washington, D.C.: Freedom House, 2013.

Hassan, Fareed M. *Tunisia: Understanding Successful Socioeconomic Development.* Washington D.C.: World Bank, 2005.

Hassim, Shireen. "Democratization: A View from Africa." *Signs: Journal of Women in Culture and Society* 31, no. 4 (2006): 928–932.

Junge, Daniel, and Siatta Scott Johnson. *Iron Ladies of Liberia*, DVD. New York: Women Make Movies, 2007.

Maathai, Wangari. "Wangari Maathai." In *Speak Truth to Power: Human Rights Defenders Who Are Changing Our World*, edited by Kerry Kennedy, pp. 38–43. New York: Crown Publishers, 2000.

———. "Nobel Lecture." Oslo City Hall, Oslo, December 10, 2004.

Mandela, Nelson. "Presidential Inaugural Address." Union Buildings, Pretoria, May 11, 1994.

Obasanjo, Olusegun. "The Elements of Democracy in Africa." In *Elements of Democracy*, edited by Olusegun Obasanjo and Akin Mabogunje, pp. 59–62. Abeokuta, Nigeria: Africa Leadership Forum Publications, 1992.

Posel, Deborah. "What's in a Name? Racial Categorisations under Apartheid and Their Afterlife." *Transformation* (2001): 50–74.

Progress of the World's Women: In Pursuit of Justice. New York: UN Women, 2011.

Sirleaf, Ellen Johnson. "Presidential Inaugural Address." Capitol Grounds, Monrovia, January 16, 2006.

Tripp, Aili Mari, et al. *African Women's Movements: Changing Political Landscapes.* Cambridge, U.K.: Cambridge University Press, 2009.

Young, Crawford. "Africa: An Interim Balance Sheet." *Journal of Democracy* 7, no. 3 (1996): 53–68.

SUGGESTED READINGS/FILMS/WEBSITES

Bauer, Gretchen, and Hannah Evelyn Britton, eds. *Women in African Parliaments.* Boulder, Colo.: Lynne Rienner, 2006.

Clark, Nancy L., and William H. Worger. *South Africa: The Rise and Fall of Apartheid.* New York: Routledge, 2013.

Dallaire, Romeo, and Samantha Power. *Shake Hands with the Devil: The Failure of Humanity in Rwanda.* New York: Carroll & Graf Publishers, 2004.

Korany, Bahgat, and Rabab El-Mahdi, eds. *The Arab Spring in Egypt: Revolution and Beyond.* Cairo: The American University in Cairo Press, 2012.

Krog, Antjie. *Country of My Skull: Guilt, Sorrow, and the Limits of Forgiveness in the New South Africa.* New York: Broadway Books, 2000.

Lesch, David W., and Mark L. Haas, eds. *The Arab Spring: Change and Resistance in the Middle East.* Boulder, Colo.: Westview Press, 2012.

Maathai, Wangari. *Unbowed: A Memoir.* New York: Alfred A. Knopf, 2006.

Mamdani, Mahmood. *When Victims Become Killers: Colonialism, Nativism, and the Genocide in Rwanda.* Princeton, N.J.: Princeton University Press, 2002.

Mandela, Nelson. *Long Walk to Freedom.* New York: Back Bay Books, 1995.

Merton, Lisa, and Alan Dater. *Taking Root: The Vision of Wangari Maathai,* DVD. New York: New Day Films, 2008.

Economics

African democratization is meant to stimulate transformation not just in the continent's political landscape, but also in the economic and social landscapes. Conventional wisdom suggests that if countries democratize, Africans will see real and positive changes in their ability to live under a representative government and participate in a more balanced and improved economic system. But the connection between democratization and economic stability and growth may be more complex than that. Some observers of Africa's political and economic transformations over the past thirty years note that changes that occur first in economic systems may help push the democratization process forward, suggesting that not only does democratization *cause* economic growth, but thriving economies may actually *stimulate* the democratization process. The goals that democratization are meant to achieve relate directly to economic matters, and during the last few decades, Africans have emphasized the necessity of good governance to help bring further economic progress to their countries. Indeed, it would seem that democratization and economic stability are increasingly connected. Journalist Pascal Fletcher frames this discussion of the interrelated nature of stable governments and strong economic growth as a natural consequence of African politics coming of age. He argues that political maturity and an increasing number of young Africans ready to work and spend money will combine to help stimulate an economic boom in Africa.[1]

Perhaps what best bridges economics and politics and exemplifies the relationship between economic development and democratization is new technology. Technology and Africans' ability to access it, particularly in terms of communication through cell phones and social media, demonstrate the link between economic growth and democratization. As noted in an *Economist* article, widespread communications technology means that "Political campaigns no longer depend on government-owned media or the ability to travel to far-flung places. They can reach voters directly and remotely via the internet, and, especially, the ubiquitous mobile telephone. They can expose political skullduggery and also tabulate poll results instantaneously, making fraud easier to detect."[2] As social media and mass communication become a reality for millions of Africans, we can expect to see both economic and political transformations driven by access to technology. At the same time, however, Africans will need to determine which types of technology best serve their countries and communities and make tough decisions about where national investment and their personal expenditure should go. Projects to bring solar-powered laptops and cell phone towers to rural communities may lead to the abandonment of less technologically exciting projects, such as well digging and vocational training programs, despite the need for clean water and employment skills. African governments and communities will need to determine which activities will best serve economically vulnerable populations.

Although many African countries experienced encouraging increases in gross domestic product (GDP) of around 5 percent annually over the past decade, the last thirty years were economically tumultuous and threatened economic security and growth. Natural disasters, such as drought and failed crops, insecurity in global markets, human health catastrophes, resource wars, and world economic crises often undermined the viability and progress of Africa's financial sectors, which of course placed Africans in vulnerable positions. The response to some of these larger threats to African economies often came from

---

[1] Pascal Fletcher. "Analysis: Africa Rise Pays Out Dividends for Democracy." *Reuters*, March 5, 2013.

[2] "African Democracy: A Glass Half- Full." *The Economist*, March 31, 2012.

external sources. The 1980s and 90s ushered in a period of foreign aid activity dominated by the Structural Adjustment Program (SAP) model. By the early 2000s, many conceded the failure of SAPs, while simultaneously a new aid model emerged as China, and to a lesser degree Japan, experimented with an industrialization investment model of foreign aid. One of the biggest threats to Africa's current economic gains is the incredible debt burden many countries carry from loans acquired during the 1970s, 80s, and 90s. The statistics are staggering. According to historian Frederick Cooper, debt has crippled African national budgets since the 1980s, when countries had "to devote an increasing percentage of export revenues to debt repayment, leaving little for necessary imports, let alone for investment. Uganda devoted 5 percent of its exports to debt service in 1980, and 66 percent around 1990; Kenya's debt service went from 16 percent of exports to 35 percent, and Cote D'Ivoire's [Ivory Coast's] from 25 percent to 60 percent" (Cooper, 2002, p. 115). Many governments then took out more loans in an effort to cover the costs of interest repayments. It is thus easy to understand why so many economists and politicians are declaring aid a failure.

Despite the continuing problem of debt from foreign aid, there are some glimmers of hope. There have been positive trends in economic progress over the past decade. Although a significant portion of Africa's GDP comes from exporting natural resources such as oil, agricultural products, and minerals, African economies are slowly diversifying. By developing other sectors, Africa will be less beholden to international markets and commodity prices that determine the value of Africa's natural resources. While more than 30 percent of Africa's growth is generated by the sale of commodities, the rest of the economy—and its growth—is based on increasing attention to other sectors, such as telecommunications, manufacturing, retail, tourism, and transportation. Botswana serves as an example of this changing economic landscape, where countries strive for economic diversification. Under former president Festus Gontebanye Mogae, Botswana's government established the Business and Economic Advisory Council, which was tasked with figuring out ways to move away from an economy based solely on diamond exports. Mogae and his advisers recognized that diamonds, though profitable, were a nonrenewable resource and thus the country needed to build an economy that was not dependent on income from that commodity. The path to economic diversification has been rocky, but Botswana's government shows signs of continuing commitment to figuring out how to develop a strong economy that will survive without revenue from the diamond industry. Such change will not be rapid, but the fact that governments are thinking about long-term economic development suggests that there is increasing awareness that natural resources with high value today may not be lucrative or available in the future.

On a micro-level, financial stability is still elusive for most Africans. Even with statistics demonstrating Africa's modest economic gains over the past decade, poverty continues to plague the continent. The economic challenges of the 1980s and 90s persist today and threaten the financial security of Africans on a daily basis. Zambian economist Dambisa Moyo explains the disappointing reality that "With an average per capita income of roughly $1 a day, sub-Saharan Africa remains the poorest region in the world. Africa's real per capita income today is lower than in the 1970s, leaving many African countries at least as poor as they were 40 years ago" (Moyo, 2009, p. 5). Foreign aid, although in principle aimed at alleviating poverty among Africa's population, has had no significant effect on helping poor Africans find financial stability and security. Policy experts agree that in order for poverty to decrease, annual GDP growth must exceed current rates. This would provide the capital necessary to ensure that resources are allocated in meaningful ways to impoverished populations. Of course, good governance is also a crucial component in poverty reduction, as governments take responsibility for using GDP growth for a greater common good. Many critics of foreign aid models argue that external attempts to stimulate economic growth while nurturing good governance have failed and have made the future of African countries bleaker by imposing bad economic policies and burdening recipient nations with crippling debt. Many questions still remain. How will African countries sustain and increase current economic growth rates? How will they continue to diversify their economic sectors? And will revenue be used more effectively to substantially reduce poverty?

This chapter examines the relationship between economic growth and democratization by focusing on some of Africa's most pressing economic challenges and transformative activities of the past three decades. Although there is evidence to suggest that foreign aid has in some ways served to promote democracy in Africa, is the reverse also true? Has democracy, as a condition of foreign aid, actually promoted economic development on the continent? This relationship is not necessarily as straightforward as some might think, for many so-called democratic countries have suffered from weak economic growth, just as some nondemocratic societies have enjoyed economic prosperity. Through a closer examination of the politics of foreign aid, debt relief, Chinese investment in Africa, and resource wars, the case studies that make up the remainder of this chapter help us begin to unpack this difficult question.

STRUCTURAL ADJUSTMENT IN AFRICA

African political security was significantly undermined by a severe economic crisis that plagued the continent in the late 1970s. Robert McNamara, then president of the World Bank, called for the establishment of a commission that would identify the causes of growing inequality between the Global North and South and proposed potential solutions to them. Under the leadership of former German chancellor Willy Brandt, the Independent Commission on International Development Issues released a report in March 1980 recommending that wealthier countries in the North transfer resources to the more impoverished countries of the South in order to create a new kind of global security. This was not charity as much as it was recognition of the dualistic nature of their relationship. Countries in the Global North depended on those in the Global South for their wealth, just as those in the South depended on those in the North for their development. Bringing an end to the economic crisis was therefore in everyone's best interests.

Several months after the Brandt Commission issued their report, a number of African leaders drafted a plan under the auspices of the Organization of African Unity to promote economic development and self-reliance among member states. In the preamble to the Lagos Plan for Action, they clearly articulated why a new development approach was necessary:

> The effect of unfulfilled promises of global development strategies has been more sharply felt in Africa than in the other continents of the world. Indeed, rather than result in an improvement in the economic situation of the continent, successive strategies have made it stagnate and become more susceptible than other regions to the economic and social crises suffered by the industrialized countries. Thus, Africa is unable to point to any significant growth rate, or satisfactory index of general well-being, in the past 20 years. Faced with this situation, and determined

to undertake measures for the basic restructuring of the economic base of our continent, we resolved to adopt a far-reaching regional approach based primarily on collective self-reliance. (Organization of African Unity, 1980, p. 4)

Officials at the World Bank criticized this plan because it did not pay sufficient attention to economic reform and private sector development. They commissioned Elliot Berg, an influential economist, to carry out a study of development in sub-Saharan Africa. In his final report he recommended that African governments move away from state-run economies and toward free market systems. The World Bank and the International Monetary Fund (IMF) therefore began placing conditions on all aid given to African countries. These conditional aid packages were known as Structural Adjustment Programs. Some of the more common loan preconditions required that governments balance their budgets, cut social spending, eliminate subsidies, provide concessions to multinational corporations to encourage investment, privatize government agencies, promote cash crop production, and retrench redundant public servants. These austerity measures allowed governments to save money so that they could more easily service their external debts. Once most African leaders realized that direct aid would not be forthcoming, they reluctantly agreed to these reforms.

Not surprisingly, structural adjustment resulted in massive hardships for most Africans. After government subsidies were eliminated, prices for food, fuel, and other basic necessities skyrocketed. High prices were coupled with the introduction of a value-added tax on most goods and services, which meant that ordinary consumers shouldered the bulk of the tax burden. Cost-recovery programs in the health and education sectors also created tremendous hardships for the poor. Those who were unable to pay were no longer able to receive healthcare or to send their children to school. Widespread retrenchment policies also created unprecedented levels of unemployment, which simply increased poverty among the masses.

Structural adjustment policies had a particularly negative effect on African women and girls. Since women are frequently responsible for food provision, the elimination of subsidies and the move toward cash crop production made it difficult for many to provide food for their families. The privatization of social services also made health and education unaffordable for the poor. Women's reproductive labor burdens often increased as they attempted to compensate for these cutbacks. In Malawi, for instance, if a clinic was compelled to introduce user fees to offset the loss of government subsidies, a peasant farmer might be unable to bring her sick child to the doctor. She would have to provide care at home, which in turn, compromised her ability to care for the rest of her family and jeopardized her child's chance of recovery. If this same woman was unable to pay her children's school fees, she might decide to keep her daughters at home so that they could help with domestic and agricultural activities. This would significantly decrease their future earning potential and increase the likelihood that they would be married off at an earlier age, a harmful practice for a host of additional reasons.

Because of these and other problems, the World Bank and the IMF began moving away from structural adjustment and toward poverty-reduction programs in the late 1990s. They believed that if African countries had greater ownership in the restructuring process, their reforms would be more successful. Lenders now encourage borrowing countries to draft Poverty Reduction Strategy Papers in consultation with local governments and civil society groups. Although these papers are supposed to lay out local investment priorities, they are often strikingly similar to the original SAPs. Critics have argued that this is because the banks, and the countries that fund them, have remained overly involved in the policy-making process. This suggests that political democratization does not necessarily open up the space for meaningful economic liberation.

DEBT RELIEF

As African states shoulder the burden of failed structural adjustment policies, an increasing number of critics are making public calls for debt forgiveness. Celebrities such as Bono and George Clooney publicly endorse debt relief, pushing the discussion onto a global stage and creating more pressure on donor countries and institutions to seriously consider writing off loans paid out to African countries. Advocates in favor of debt relief as a corrective policy argue that African countries were subjected to aid programs that not only failed to stimulate development but actually set recipient countries back economically because of the crippling interest rates and enormous loan repayments. Although SAPs of the 1980s and 1990s are the focal point of the push for debt relief, critics of foreign aid in Africa point to a long history of failed experiments in African aid and contend that much of Africa's current suffering is the result of over fifty years of bad foreign aid policy.

The rhetoric driving debate on debt forgiveness goes deeper than simply absolving Africa of loan repayment. The discourse illuminates the complicated history of aid, or, more precisely, the history of the failure of aid. Estimates suggest that up to $600 billion has been given as aid to Africa in the last forty to fifty years (Akonor, 2008). Presumably, if aid worked as it was designed to, African countries would not continue to need to appeal for more aid, yet many countries are repeat recipients, and in worst-case scenarios, some of those countries have received more aid to pay for older loans. Borrowing more money to pay for already borrowed money indicates a serious problem in the aid/development model.

Debt relief, although an increasingly popular *cause célèbre*, is not a concept or practice born out of just the last few years. In the mid-1990s, the World Bank began refinancing old loans in order to make repayment possible. In 1998, and then again in 2005, donor countries agreed to write off approximately $90 billion. In 1996, the World Bank and the IMF implemented the Heavily Indebted Poor Countries (HIPC) Initiative to significantly reduce debt repayment in thirty-six countries, of which thirty were African. Subsequent programs stemming from the HIPC Initiative followed in later years to continue the efforts to stave off the collapse of African economies. However, the call to wipe out Africa's debt has intensified in the last decade, and a growing number of policy makers, economists, and celebrities from around the world have made it a point of global debate. The issue of debt relief is complicated, and there are no clear-cut answers on how to proceed. As one former World Bank official posits, there is a difference between forgiving debt and making debt manageable, and there are ethical ramifications for forgiving countries completely of their debt obligations because it leaves no culpability for governments who abused the aid and provides little incentive for future leaders to wisely utilize it (Calderisi, 2007, pp. 27–28). Historian Frederick Cooper pushes deeper into the discourse on foreign aid failures, debt relief, and its consequences in his consideration of how old debt plagues younger generations in Africa and who is to blame for the heavy debt burden. He explains:

> We are caught in a dilemma: on the one hand is the fact that young Africans are saddled with the multiple costs of the illegitimate rulers who built up big debts and bad structures. On the other hand, the writing off of debt encourages irresponsibility. . . . If a new generation of Africans is to get out of the difficulties their elders—with lots of help from the outside—got them into, all of us need to take a more balanced

view of responsibility. Let us realize that international banking, transnational corporations, donor agencies, and international institutions are not some impersonal embodiment of the 'world economy' but are specific institutions, particular kinds of power relations, and they should be scrutinized just as carefully as the behavior of African politicians. (Cooper, 2002, p. 203)

Thus, the link between mishandled aid and bad governance becomes only one part of the equation, as the international community is forced to also accept partial blame for its failings and all parties involved seek solutions on how to move the continent forward and beyond the staggering debt burden.

By the turn of the twenty-first century, despite some critics' opposition to debt relief, major efforts were made to ease the economic obligations caused by foreign aid packages from the past. Moving beyond the paradigm of debt reduction, a new era of debt forgiveness was born. With the backing of the G8 countries, the IMF, the World Bank, and the African Development Fund, a series of Multilateral Debt Relief Initiatives (MDRIs) were passed in 2005 and 2006 that extended the HIPC process to result in debt cancellation, not just reduction. The MDRI approach continues to dominate the trajectory of debt forgiveness and is now considered an instrumental factor in the potential for African countries to reach the Millennium Development Goals (MDGs) established by the United Nations. The idea is that the less debt these countries have to repay, the more money they will have freed up to work on improving living conditions and to invest in their countries' emerging economic sectors. Adding momentum to the debt forgiveness model, Brazil's president announced at the 2013 African Union fifty-year anniversary celebration her decision to write off $900 million in loans from Brazil to various African countries. Although the long-term consequences of debt cancellation remain to be seen, it would seem that most policymakers today consider the debt burden of African countries to be too debilitating and are moving toward a policy of forgiving Africans and their governments for the loans acquired by the previous generation.

CHINESE INVESTMENT AND AID

One of the most hotly discussed topics within discourse on contemporary African economic development is the role of China's investments and partnerships on the continent. China's history in contemporary

African economies goes as far back as World War II but saw fresh momentum as countries gained independence in the 1960s. By the 1970s China was an emerging economic partner in African development and commerce. Over the past thirty years China's growing involvement in African economic activity has laid the framework for a different approach to foreign aid in a continent where the Global North's model of aid shows few signs of sustainable success. The ideological differences between China and the Global North may be best explained as a consequence of China's position as a fellow developing country that has managed to increase economic production and significantly decrease poverty. Those two goals, of course, represent the heart of what foreign aid is intended to do in Africa, but thus far the results have been less than satisfactory. China's experience in self-development profoundly shapes that nation's approach to aid and investment in Africa, and a growing number of observers are reporting that China's model may work better than foreign aid packages from countries and institutions in the Global North.

FIGURE 2.1   Senegalese children welcome Chinese President Hu Jintao to their country in early 2009. Hosted by Senegalese President Abdoulaye Wade, President Jintao toured the construction site that would become a national theater. The project was financed by China and serves as a reminder of their growing presence in Africa. Photograph by SEYLLOU/AFP/Getty Images.

China uses more of an investment model of aid than a gift-giving approach. In other words, China views African nations as potential partners, and as such, both China and African countries should see returns on their economic collaboration. Consequently, China's activities in Africa are specific and typically involve close Chinese oversight and continual involvement. The projects China initiates are forecast to be profitable and often serve the economic development goals of China, not just Africa. As Deborah Brautigam (2011) explains in her research about China in Africa, the Chinese aid model is different from the aid given by the Global North because it emphasizes developing infrastructure and increasing production in specific sectors. China does not dump money into Africa, but instead envisions aid as part of a larger economic investment policy. Another key difference between China's aid and aid from the Global North is that China's aid does not come with stipulations about African partner governments meeting demands for democratic and economic reform. While the Global North often requires African recipient governments to promise to conform to Western models of democracy and economic practices, China has no interest in interfering with Africa's political and commercial systems. For African leaders resistant to European and American imposition, China's indifference to their political and economic practices is particularly refreshing. China is responsible for infusing an ever-increasing amount of money into African countries. The Chinese invested $20 million in Africa in 1975. By 2004, that number had increased to $900 million, demonstrating the intensifying Sino-African relationship (Moyo, 2009, p. 103).

The benefits for China are clear—it gains access to African resources and ensures the extraction of those resources by promoting infrastructure projects. China desperately needs these resources, which include oil and minerals, to provide for its domestic markets. It would seem that there are also obvious advantages to African countries receiving China's investment and aid. Rather than seeing aid money tied up in projects conceived by the Global North, Africans quickly see signs of increased economic activity shortly after partnerships with the Chinese are formalized. There is particularly strong momentum in Africa's manufacturing sectors, which offer tangible results in the form of jobs and finished products. The Chinese bring with them skills and knowledge about construction, industrialization, and mining, and that information is transferred to Africans.

China's increasing presence throughout the continent has many outsiders and some Africans nervous, as many question if China is the

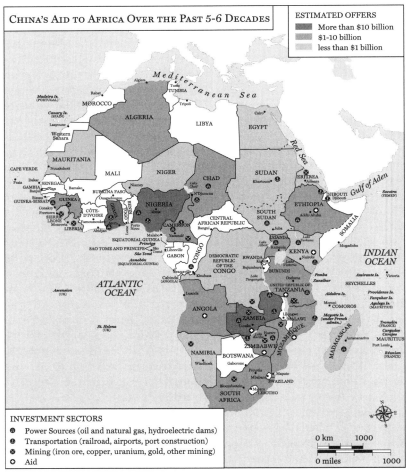

MAP 2.1   China's aid to Africa over the past 5-6 decades

new imperial power and what that might mean for the future of the Global North's relationship with Africa. Opponents of China's evolving engagement in African economies worry that the Chinese minimalist approach will undermine their efforts to develop aid packages that are meant to bring profits to European and American partners and allow the Global North to dictate the terms of Africa's economic and political activities. China is most interested in industrial projects, but large-scale industrialization is absent from most plans devised by donors from the Global North. There is also great concern from Africans and outsiders alike about China's poor human rights record and exploitative labor practices spreading into its partner countries. There is already increasing tension between African workers and Chinese managers and skilled laborers brought in to run collaborative projects. African workers claim they are underpaid or even unpaid and subjected to long hours and unsafe working conditions and that they are blocked from obtaining skilled labor positions in order to keep those jobs open for Chinese workers. These conflicts have already boiled over, and there have been sporadic incidents of violence between African and Chinese workers. Finally, there is anxiety about China gaining a stronghold over many of Africa's most coveted natural resources. Such a shift could profoundly alter the global distribution and consumption of the continent's products. Despite all the anxiety and opposition to China's involvement in Africa, however, it is clear that China and many of its African partners envision a long and fruitful relationship into the future.

VIOLENCE AND THE "RESOURCE CURSE"

In 1979 the American oil company Chevron discovered "black gold" in southern Sudan in the province of Western Upper Nile, an area that is now known as Unity State in the newly independent country of South Sudan. Several years later they discovered even larger oil deposits in a nearby region. The Sudanese government, in conjunction with Chevron, Royal Dutch Shell, and the Arab Petroleum Investments Corporation, formed the White Nile Petroleum Company to construct a pipeline from the Sudanese oil fields to Port Sudan on the Red Sea. When civil war broke out in 1983, sparked in large part by the discovery of oil and the government's abrogation of an earlier peace agreement granting southern provinces limited autonomy, Chevron suspended its operations in Sudan. The government, however, moved forward with its plans to construct a pipeline. In fact, they used an array of scorched earth tactics to ensure that nothing would threaten the country's oil development. The state deployed armed militias, Antonov bombers, and helicopter gunships to terrorize the civilian population. They did not act alone, since various multinational oil companies were also complicit in the violence and displacement, providing the Sudanese government with revenue to purchase powerful military equipment.

In 2005, after twenty-two years of warfare and the death of more than 2 million civilians, the government signed a Comprehensive Peace Agreement with the Sudanese People's Liberation Army, the main rebel group in the conflict between north and south. (Ironically, the peace negotiations inspired a different group of rebels in the Darfur region of western Sudan to take up arms against the state in 2003. Their major grievance was not oil, but instead, access to grazing land.) Under the terms of the Agreement, the state promised to hold a referendum after six years in which the citizens of the south could confirm Sudan's unity or vote for secession. In January 2011, a referendum was held and the vast majority voted for independence, which was officially granted on July 9, 2011. At the time of writing, the oil-rich border region of Abyei remains heavily contested and has been claimed by both sides.

The major historical question raised by the Sudanese case study is whether the presence of natural resources helps or hinders a country's economic development. In other words, is there such a thing as a "resource curse"? Many scholars argue that countries with an

FIGURE 2.2   A Sudanese family sets up shelter in Bredjing Refugee Camp in eastern Chad. This camp, along with several others in the region, is a place where people fleeing Darfur sought safety and relied on outside aid for survival. Unfortunately, life in these camps was far from stable, as refugees found themselves struggling for supplies and were often subjected to violence. Photograph by Christoph Bangert, ca 2008.

abundance of nonrenewable natural resources do in fact suffer from economic underdevelopment and weak state institutions at a much higher rate than those that are relatively resource poor. Because they are able to earn significant revenue from the extraction of oil or gems, rulers of these nations have had little incentive to develop relationships with their citizenry. Warlords and rebel groups also find ways of exploiting certain types of natural resources in order to finance their military and political activities. Small, high-value commodities such as diamonds and coltan are particularly valuable. Because much of this trade is extralegal and does not support large-scale development, resource abundance is often seen as an "economic curse."

Resources can also be seen as a "political curse" in that they have prompted secession movements. In addition to the protracted struggle that resulted in the eventual independence of South Sudan, violent resource-based wars of secession have taken place in a number of African countries, including the Democratic Republic of the Congo (Katanga, 1960–1963), Nigeria (Biafra, 1967–1970), and Angola (Cabinda, 1960–present). Besides triggering all manner of political violence, the plundering of scarce resources can also prolong and exacerbate conflicts. In the 1990s and early 2000s, for instance, "blood diamonds" fueled brutal civil wars in both Liberia and Sierra Leone, resulting in the deaths of tens of thousands of civilians and combatants, many of whom were young children. They have also been used to fund violent conflicts in Angola, Ivory Coast, and the Democratic Republic of the Congo. In an effort to halt the spread of illicit diamonds, the international community launched the Kimberley Process Certification Scheme in 2003, which requires governments to certify all diamond exports to ensure that they were not obtained from conflict zones. Unfortunately, the effectiveness of the certification process has been called into question in recent years, and a number of former proponents have withdrawn their support from the scheme.

It is important to mention that an abundance of resources does not necessarily mean that a country will suffer from conflict or poverty. If a country has a stable economy and a relatively strong government, it has the potential to prosper from its resources. Botswana is rich in diamonds, and yet it has never experienced armed conflict or political violence. When diamonds were discovered in 1967, one year after independence from Great Britain, the government began putting their profits to good use within the public sector. They used diamond revenues to provide education and healthcare to all citizens, unlike neighboring Zimbabwe, where state officials embezzled profits to prop up the corrupt regime of Robert Mugabe. Unlike most sub-Saharan African countries where gross domestic product averaged just over $2,300 per capita in 2011, Botswana's diamond wealth has brought relative prosperity to the country. The World Bank estimates that their rate of GDP was $14,746 per person. This suggests that resources do not have to be a "curse" to Africans, particularly if they are coupled with good governance and meaningful public investment.

CONCLUSION

Intricately connected to concepts of good governance and democratization are the issues of economic growth and development. It is not enough for Africans to hope for increased economic production, whether it is from aid, debt relief, Chinese investment, or the exploitation of natural resources. They must not only be able to hear or read about the latest factory being built, mine being established, or aid package coming into their countries; they must also start to *feel* the impact of those activities. For Africans straddled with the failure and debt of early postcolonial economic initiatives and loans, it is increasingly critical that individuals see tangible proof that the economies in their countries are succeeding. Throughout Africa's cities and countryside, it is easy to find half-started, abandoned construction projects. Most Africans live on meager incomes and account for much of the world's poorest populations while they live in the shadow of some of the world's most valuable resources. Conversations about democratization may very well seem hollow to people who are more concerned with feeding their families and paying rent, but good governance determines whether resources and/or aid will be utilized to better the lives of private citizens. The question of whether good governance ultimately comes from a democratic political system or could be an element of an alternative political system is still debated, but what remains clear is that Africans will continue to search for opportunities to improve their economic status and that their financial livelihoods will continue to be affected by the choices—both good and bad—that their governments make.

REFERENCES

Akonor, Kwame. "Foreign Aid to Africa: A Hollow Hope?" *International Law and Politics* 40 (2008): 1071–1078.

Brautigam, Deborah. *The Dragon's Gift: The Real Story of China in Africa.* New York: Oxford University Press, 2011.

Calderisi, Robert. *The Trouble with Africa: Why Foreign Aid Isn't Working.* New York: Macmillan, 2007.

Cooper, Frederick. *Africa since 1940: The Past of the Present.* Cambridge, U.K.: Cambridge University Press, 2002.

Independent Commission on International Development Issues. *North-South: Programme for Survival.* London: Pan Books, 1980.

Leke, Acha, et al. "What's Driving Africa's Growth?" New York: McKinsey and Company, June 2010.

Moyo, Dambisa. *Dead Aid: Why Aid Is Not Working and How There Is a Better Way for Africa.* New York: Farrar, Straus and Giroux, 2009.

Organization of African Unity. *The Lagos Plan of Action for the Economic Development of Africa.* Addis Ababa, Ethiopia: World Bank, July 1980.

World Bank. *Accelerated Development in Sub-Saharan Africa: An Agenda for Action.* Washington, D.C.: World Bank, 1981.

————. *World Development Indicators Database.* Washington, D.C.: World Bank, 2013.

SUGGESTED READINGS/FILMS/WEBSITES

Brummel, Bill, June Molgaard, and Jeffrey Wright. *Blood Diamonds*, DVD. The History Channel, 2006.

Habila, Helon. *Oil on Water: A Novel.* New York: W.W. Norton and Company, 2011.

Patey, Luke Anthony. "State Rules: Oil Companies and Armed Conflict in Sudan." *Third World Quarterly* 28, no. 5 (2007): 997–1016.

————. "Crude Days Ahead? Oil and the Resource Curse in Sudan." *African Affairs* 109, no. 437 (2010): 617–636.

Peel, Michael. *A Swamp Full of Dollars: Pipelines and Paramilitaries at Nigeria's Oil Frontier.* Chicago: Lawrence Hill Books, 2010.

Rotberg, Robert I., ed. *China into Africa: Trade, Aid, and Influence.* Cambridge, Mass.: World Peace Foundation (Brookings Institution), 2008.

Smillie, Ian. *Blood on the Stone Greed, Corruption and War in the Global Diamond Trade.* London: Anthem Press, 2010.

Thomas-Emeagwali, Gloria. *Women Pay the Price: Structural Adjustment in Africa and the Caribbean.* Trenton, N.J.: Africa World Press, 1995.

Van Soest, Landon. *Good Fortune*, DVD. PBS Films, 2010.

3

Health and Healing

In April 2001 the leaders of member states of the African Union (AU) made a public pledge that their governments would allocate 15 percent of their national budgets to promote public health initiatives, policies, and education. The Abuja Declaration highlighted the great need for African nations to improve their healthcare sectors and put pressure on African governments to include healthcare as a national priority. This pledge was motivated by a global initiative to improve the living and working conditions of the world's poorest people. The Millennium Declaration, adopted by 189 heads of state in September 2000, was comprised of a list of eight goals, known as the Millennium Development Goals (MDGs), aimed at alleviating challenges faced by impoverished people living in the so-called developing world. Among those goals, three focused specifically on public health: MDG 4, Reduce Child Deaths; MDG 5, Improve Maternal Health; and MDG 6, Combat AIDS and Malaria. Although this was a worldwide effort, the Abuja Declaration was an important African initiative that demonstrated the compliance and collaboration of AU members to work with the global community on fulfilling the MDGs.

It is revealing that the beginning of the millennium ushered in a renewed commitment to public health from parties both inside and outside of Africa, which serves as a reminder that previous initiatives had failed or at minimum had not been strong enough to absorb contemporary health crises in Africa, such as the HIV/AIDS pandemic. One of the promises given by the leaders of newly independent African countries was to develop better healthcare systems and to improve living conditions. By the early 2000s it was obvious that the promises made in the early postcolonial period had not materialized and that in some ways, healthcare and health crises were much bigger problems that Africans faced. That these crises intensified parallel to governmental experiments in public health policy and practices and slowly unfolding democratization of some governments is no coincidence. Public health inextricably relates to democratization and other political trajectories. Healthcare and wellness are focal points for many leaders, regardless of their ideological approaches to governance. Good governance can contribute to improved health and care, while bad governance may lead to a general demise in wellness and treatment, thus suggesting that one of the biggest threats to African public health is not necessarily the diseases and conditions themselves but the resources allocated—in appropriate and efficient ways—to combat public health threats. Paradoxically, we may also view public health crises as threats to fragile governments and economies, making it even more difficult for governments to respond in useful ways. The democratization of public health initiatives might actually be hindered by the health crises that threaten to destabilize delicately burgeoning democracies and tenuous economies. As discussed later in this chapter, major health crises such as HIV/AIDS clearly affected socioeconomic conditions throughout southern and eastern Africa over the last thirty years, coinciding with a period of political turmoil and transformation. The result is that although promises were made to improve access to health and the quality of health care in the 1970s and 80s, it is evident that African governments fell short of reaching those goals and in the 2000s face intensifying public health challenges.

Indeed, African leaders of newly independent states focused on healthcare initiatives as major components of their campaign platforms, but these agendas were sensitive to the language of decolonization. There was an emphasis on expanding healthcare and promoting wellness among Africans in ways that blended African realities with Westernized concepts of health. Just as Africans during the late twentieth century sought to Africanize the democratization process, so too did they consider the importance of Africanizing health systems. In 1971 Tanzanian president Julius Nyerere included an overview of the status of health and healthcare in his report about the state of the country at the ten-year anniversary of independence. Although he cited many examples of the improvements in healthcare under his leadership, Nyerere highlighted the significant challenge of Africanizing concepts of health and illness. Part of the process of liberating Africa from its colonial legacies was to develop Africanized ideologies, policies, and practices, which included African approaches to public health. Nyerere conceded that despite the statistics demonstrating decreasing rates of communicable diseases, increasing numbers of doctors and clinics, and overall greater numbers of Tanzanians accessing healthcare, there was still much to be done to improve the healthcare system of the country. Nyerere urged his country to

> 'think Tanzanian' in relation to health as in other things. It is no use our laying such high standards of building, sanitation, and equipment for our rural health centres etc., that we can only afford to build one or two a year instead of the hundreds which are needed. What is important to our people is that they should have services available; they don't need palaces. It doesn't matter if these services are available in a mud hut, provided that this hut is kept scrupulously clean, that light and air can get through it, that it has clean water available, and some means of sterilising thermometers and other instruments. . . . [A]ll the time we must be concerned to see how cheaply we can provide the basic facilities and not how beautiful they look to visiting Presidents or tourists. . . . We cannot afford to provide facilities for a few people to get advanced treatment for special heart disease while the masses of our people are not able to get treatment for the common diseases which make their lives a misery. That is a hard doctrine, but it is a question of priorities. (TANU, 1971, p. 29)

Nyerere and other African leaders sought to develop and implement plans that were appropriate to the African context while also meeting the increasing demands of citizens for widespread healthcare.

    This approach suggests that there must also be consideration for African understandings and practices of healing. Although the last thirty years of African healthcare discourse centered on medical practices from the Global North, there has been a small but vocal group of health and social workers who speak about the importance of allowing Africans to determine what is and is not healthy and what does and does not constitute healing. They criticize the massive amounts of foreign and national money allocated for healthcare to implement inappropriate systems of health education and medical care. Some of them argue that perhaps one of the most critical issues in addressing African public health is that outside influence obscures African traditions and approaches to wellness and healing and is thus set up to fail.

Starting in the 1970s and 80s, citizens of young, independent African countries expected their leaders to produce tangible results of all their revolution and election promises, including within the realm of healthcare. Instead, an economic downturn set in and many of the expensive plans to improve the health sector had to be abandoned. Historian Frederick Cooper suggests that initiatives to add more sanitation facilities, doctors, and clinics never came to fruition and, in fact, some countries still do not have as many physicians per capita as they did in the early 1970s (Cooper, 2002, p. 108). At a time when expectations were high and patience for change was running low, Africans saw colonial healthcare provisions and facilities crumble into a postcolonial demise. Unfortunately, the last few decades of the twentieth century was also a time when dramatic health crises surfaced, making the pursuit of wellness and healing even more challenging.

Where African governments failed in regard to health initiatives, two distinct responses have manifested with varying degrees of success and failure. Internally, African communities—dismayed and beleaguered not from reading the dire statistics but from actually experiencing and comprising those disheartening accounts and reports about the failure of healthcare—began filling the void themselves. Grassroots organizations and community networks have attempted to meet the needs of the continent's most vulnerable. These efforts can be seen in the orphanages caring for HIV-infected orphans, food service projects providing the sick and elderly with at least one meal a day, clinics operating with barebones staff to monitor children's wellness, midwives tending to the needs of pregnant women and newborns, and community activists going door to door to teach women and men about the dangers of unprotected sex or sleeping without mosquito nets. Such localized activities are examples of how African individuals and communities embrace a self-help ideology in times when their governments fail to meet their health and healing needs. Such grassroots responses are fraught with challenges as funding, bureaucracy, training, and facilities make it difficult for local groups to operate.

There has also been a strong external response as nongovernmental organizations, charity groups, and foreign government-funded programming attempt to ameliorate the failings of African healthcare systems. These initiatives are often in response to larger health threats, such as malaria and HIV/AIDS, but also respond to more localized or temporary issues such as waterborne illnesses, cholera outbreaks, and health concerns within refugee and internal displacement camps. Some of the external responses involve millions of dollars and strict rules for implementation, such as the U.S. HIV/AIDS funding program through the President's Emergency Plan for AIDS Relief (PEPFAR) and the malaria eradication efforts of the Bill & Melinda Gates Foundation. Others are smaller initiatives that reflect a grassroots ideology and thus take on more localized projects that require less capital, such as the HIV-prevention program "Grassroots Soccer" and small groups of surgeons and gynecologists from the Global North who use their skills and access to medical supplies to provide surgery for women suffering from fistulas or needing hysterectomies. While the external response demonstrates a global concern for the health and well-being of Africans, there are obvious problems with outsiders setting public health agendas and implementing programs. Cultural differences, donor-driven agendas, and sustainability challenges plague the projects run by foreign funds and officials.

There is also concern that with the influx of funding from outside sources, African governments have been relieved of responsibility for healthcare. Although African leaders have spoken out publicly about the importance of public health, the situation remains critical. Insiders and outsiders alike concede that healthcare is essentially a failed initiative in Africa. The Abuja Declaration and the Millennium Development Goals signaled an admission that a renewed pledge to restore and improve healthcare systems in Africa was required if the continent was to meet the health needs of its population. More than ten years on, the results show slow progress. According to statistics from 2010, South Africa and Rwanda are the only countries that have met the Abuja Declaration goal of allocating at least 15 percent of their national budget to health programming and resources. Only eight African countries are on track to fulfill the healthcare-related standards listed in the MDGs, and most African countries remain far below expectations. The amount of money spent on healthcare by African governments is shockingly low, with the median amount of real per capita government spending hovering around $14, up from $10 in 2001. African governments are not the only bodies failing to meet the guidelines established by the Abuja Declaration and the MDGs. Both plans relied on collaboration and increased financial commitment from African governments and donor nations. Subsequent agreements throughout the first decade of the twenty-first century resulted in promises of aid to reach $130 billion, but by 2009 the amount of aid received was only $27 billion. As the four case studies in this chapter clearly demonstrate, African health challenges are at critical levels, and to date, African governments and donor countries have failed to meet the needs of the threatened population.

HIV/AIDS

The HIV/AIDS crisis poses a serious challenge to African democratization efforts because of the tremendous social, political, and economic costs that have ensued. Although there have been many positive developments over the last three decades, the disease continues to ravage the continent. In 2011, the year for which the most recent statistics are available, UNAIDS reported that there were 23.5 million Africans living with HIV, the virus that causes AIDS. Roughly one in twenty adults in sub-Saharan Africa between the ages of 15 and 49 are currently infected, a number that represents 60 percent of the worldwide total. Prevalence rates in southern Africa are the highest in the world. In Swaziland, for instance, the prevalence rate is 26 percent, while Botswana and Lesotho both have rates of over 23 percent. Despite these grim statistics, the number of persons newly infected with the virus was actually 25 percent lower in 2011 than it was in 2001. Furthermore, the number of Africans dying from AIDS-related diseases has declined by 32 percent since the mid-2000s because of increased access to antiretroviral drugs (ARVs).

Although there is historical evidence to suggest that Africans have been living with HIV since the 1930s, the virus did not reach epidemic levels until the early 1980s. Along the shores of Lake Victoria in East Africa, the virus spread rapidly due to a number of interrelated factors including widespread labor migration, high rates of sexually transmitted diseases, and the low status of women, which undermined their reproductive health and decision-making power within the household (AVERT, 2013). Uganda was particularly hard hit, and by the end of the decade, HIV prevalence among pregnant women in the country's capital had peaked at over 30 percent. The disease also spread within West Africa, although it never reached epidemic proportions because regional sexual networks were not as tightly woven due to the long distances between cities and the difficulties of getting from one place to another. It did, however, manage to take hold in southern Africa, traveling rapidly down the TanZam

Highway, which connected Tanzania with Zambia. By the late 1980s, the disease had moved into Malawi, Mozambique, and the rest of the southern region, thus sparking an epidemic of devastating proportions.

Most African governments initially responded poorly to the AIDS epidemic, in large part because of the economic crisis that precipitated the move toward structural adjustment. Since treatment options were not yet available, they focused their efforts on prevention by encouraging people to *abstain* from sex, to *be faithful* to one partner, and to use *condoms* consistently and correctly (i.e., the ABC approach). Uganda is frequently cited as a country that responded quickly and effectively to the crisis. In 1987 the Ministry of Health established a national AIDS Control Program and a National Committee for the Prevention of AIDS. Together with the World Health Organization, they launched a broad-based mobilization campaign where they disseminated HIV-prevention messages throughout the country. This approach was effective in slowing the spread of the disease and became a model for much of Africa.

South Africa responded much more slowly to the epidemic. When the African National Congress replaced the apartheid government in 1994, they began restructuring their healthcare system just as the AIDS crisis was exploding. In 1998, for instance, the government stopped trials of the drug azidothymidine (AZT) to prevent mother-to-child transmission because they thought it was too expensive.

FIGURE 3.1 African governments have utilized various strategies to fight the HIV/AIDS crisis. In these billboards, one found in Kigali and the other in Kampala, we see the importance of abstinence rhetoric in state-sponsored public health campaigns. Photographs by Alicia C. Decker, 2005.

FIGURE 3.2   Improving public health is an important part of the Millennium Development Goals, but access to quality health care is limited in many African communities. Outside this camp for internally displaced persons in northern Uganda, hundreds of people stand in long lines to receive routine vaccinations. Photograph by Alicia C. Decker, 2005.

Instead, they focused their efforts on prevention campaigns. Increasingly frustrated by government inaction, a group of HIV-positive citizens in Cape Town established the Treatment Action Campaign later that year. This important organization, nominated in 2004 for a Nobel Peace Prize, has played a leading role in holding their government accountable for the delivery of healthcare services, campaigning against the denial of AIDS by the state, and challenging major pharmaceutical companies to make AIDS treatment more affordable. The latter was particularly important because effective antiretroviral therapies were priced beyond the reach of most African governments. They lobbied the drug manufacturers to allow local companies to produce the drugs themselves or to import them from other countries that were producing lower-cost generic versions. After much negotiation, the South African government was granted permission to produce and import cheap HIV drugs as long as they agreed to protect intellectual property rights.

Over the next several years, the world's largest drug companies began providing ARVs to other parts of the continent at greatly reduced prices, which has had a major impact on health outcomes. According to the World Health Organization, the number of people receiving AIDS treatment in sub-Saharan Africa increased more than twenty-fold from 100,000 in 2003 to 2.1 million in 2007. While only 2 percent of those needing drugs received them in 2003, 30 percent received them in 2007. By 2010, this number had grown to 49 percent. If 80 percent of a population that needs drugs receives them, that country has achieved "universal access." Three African countries have reached this important threshold: Botswana, Namibia, and Rwanda. It is important to recognize that these countries have also been at the forefront of democratization efforts, which suggests that large public health crises do not necessarily derail larger political projects, even if they pose significant challenges to them.

MALARIA AND TUBERCULOSIS

Africa's population faces numerous health threats, many of which stem from changing environmental conditions and migration patterns that occurred during colonial rule. Nearly three hundred infectious diseases have been identified in Africa, including malaria and tuberculosis (TB). The effects of these and other diseases such as bilharzia and sleeping sickness are particularly problematic as the health and productivity of African populations deteriorate and the cost of combating such diseases becomes a financial burden on families, communities, governments, and international donors. With other health-related crises to tend to, Africa's healthcare system and funding is stretched too thin to fully address the pervasive fight against malaria and TB. The human and monetary costs of these diseases threaten the stability and productivity of already tenuous African economies and healthcare systems.

Malaria has long been a problem in Africa, but its impact intensified under colonial expansion and postcolonial agricultural activities. As additional land was cleared for agricultural use, stagnant water allowed *Anopheles* mosquitoes carrying the parasite to thrive. Communities that had not been exposed to malaria and had little natural immunity to the disease found themselves in a transformed ecosystem and especially susceptible to malaria. Although preventative measures and treatment options are available, many Africans have found it difficult to pay for and access such resources. As a result, malaria continues to be one of the largest health challenges in contemporary Africa. According to an MDG report published in 2012, 174 million Africans were infected with malaria in 2010. The UN reports an average of roughly 880,000 deaths per year due to malaria. Africa carries a heavy burden in terms of the disease. Over 60 percent of malaria cases each year occur in African countries, and a staggering 91 percent of deaths from malaria take place in sub-Saharan Africa. The elderly, people infected with HIV/AIDS, pregnant women, and children under the age of five are especially vulnerable to this disease. Despite malaria being a long-term problem with identified prevention and treatment methods, an extremely large number of Africans continue to be affected by the disease.

In an effort to eradicate or at least significantly reduce the number of cases of malaria, a major collaborative initiative called Roll Back Malaria was launched in 1998. Partners included the World Health Organization (WHO), the United Nations Children's Fund (UNICEF), the United Nations Development Program (UNDP), and the World Bank, as well as nongovernmental organizations, national ministries of health, research institutes, and the private sector. By 2010, there were nearly five hundred partners participating in the program, all working toward the goals laid out by the Global Malaria Action Plan. This multifaceted approach involves education, prevention, and treatment. Another important contributor to the fight against malaria is the Bill & Melinda Gates Foundation. As part of the global effort to reduce malaria-related deaths, this foundation has committed over $3 billion to the research and development of better diagnostics, potential vaccines, and more effective treatment options (Bill & Melinda Gates Foundation, 2013). Through the work of global initiatives and community-based programming, there are small signs of improvement but also indications that more must be done to limit the effects of this deadly disease in Africa and beyond. Although there was a 25 percent decrease in malarial deaths globally and a 33 percent decrease in malarial deaths in Africa between 2000 and 2010, organizations involved in fighting malaria had hoped to cut the mortality rate in half during that time period (Roll Back Malaria Partnership, 2013). In terms of prevention, the percentage of African children sleeping under the protection of insecticide-treated nets between 2000 and 2010 rose from 2 percent to 39 percent (UNICEF, 2013). However, researchers also note that the malaria parasite continues to rapidly evolve and develop resistance to insecticides, thus limiting the efficacy of using treated nets. Malaria eradication programs continue to face multiple challenges and huge expenses in combating this disease.

TB is another disease that persistently affects African populations. Indeed, there is evidence to suggest that the rate of infection in sub-Saharan Africa actually increased over the past twenty years. More promisingly, infection rates in North Africa declined slightly during that time period, and the number of TB deaths marginally decreased in both regions of Africa. Like malaria, TB is a preventable and often curable disease, but more education and resources must become accessible in order to see more substantial improvements in TB infection and mortality rates. TB is a leading cause of death among those infected with HIV/AIDS, so it is important to continue to successfully prevent and treat the disease in order to keep it from infecting their weakened immune systems. New initiatives to combat the disease pay close attention to the relationship between TB and HIV/AIDS, and protocols are evolving to tackle these interrelated diseases. Thus far, however, evaluations of recent programs to limit TB infections and deaths are inconclusive as to degrees of success.

The Global Fund is one of the largest organizations working on the interrelated public health crisis stemming from high incidences of malaria, TB, and HIV/AIDs. It was created with the goal of disseminating funds to countries in order to support programs to prevent, treat, and care for people suffering from these diseases. The Global Fund oversees approximately 82 percent of all money allocated to fight TB and 50 percent of that allocated to fight malaria. The amount of money needed to achieve the TB and malaria-related MDGs is astronomical. In 2009, researchers estimated that to meet malaria control goals, programming would cost at least $3.5 billion per year and that efforts to decrease the prevalence of TB would require around $4.5 billion per year. It is important to note that while the costs of malaria and TB are a substantial burden on African communities and economies, most of the money earmarked to combat these crippling infection rates comes from the international community. Only recently have we seen collaboration between foreign donors and grassroots organizations to find ways to effectively educate, prevent, and treat malaria and TB. Although it may be too late to fully achieve the goals set forth by the MDGs, it is hoped that as community-based health service initiatives connect with outside funders, more people will escape the devastating consequences of these two fatal diseases.

MATERNAL AND REPRODUCTIVE HEALTH

In 1994 Cairo hosted the International Conference on Population and Development. The conference was significant in that 179 participating countries agreed with the concept that women's healthcare needed to be rights-based. That is, in order for women to enjoy the security of human and women's rights, they had to have access to family planning and sexual and reproductive healthcare. The course set forward by the conference's approved Program of Action was controversial and perceived as radical to some because it declared that women should have access to safe abortion, contraception, control over their reproductive organs, education on sexual health, and the ability to avoid female genital cutting. While the conference was bold and aggressive in its stance that for human and women's rights to be achieved, women must be guaranteed better reproductive and maternal healthcare services, the goals of the conference failed to gain much momentum after the closing ceremony. Less than a decade later, many of the same principles put forth in the conference's Program of Action served as the foundation for the establishment of the MDG related to women's health. The threats to reproductive and maternal wellness African women face include sexually transmitted diseases (HIV/ AIDS in particular), unplanned pregnancies and lack of contraceptive options, unsafe or inaccessible abortion, infertility, cancer that affects the reproductive system, maternal and infant mortality, pregnancy complications, reproductive tract infections, and female genital cutting. The Cairo conference and subsequent development of the women's health initiatives in the MDG seek to drastically reduce or eradicate those obstacles to women's health.

Of all the MDGs, the one that shows the least improvement and progress is MDG 5, which relates to maternal and reproductive health. Women's healthcare, particularly related to reproduction, was an arena of African life that European colonizers particularly invaded. Many colonial administrators attempted to medicalize childbirth by training women to be certified nurses or licensed midwives, which in turn put pressure on community midwives and African women who were expected to change their approach to pregnancy and delivery based on ideas and values of the Global North. Although many African women resisted the medicalization of childbirth and still retain the services of local midwives, there continues to be competing ideology influencing the allocation of resources and educational emphasis when it comes to maternal health. Although that tension may continue for more generations to come, what is troubling to all involved in public health, gynecological, and obstetric care is that by 2012, 39 percent of pregnancies were unplanned, only 17 percent of married women of child-bearing age used "modern" contraception, and African women had a 1 in 31 chance of dying while pregnant or during childbirth. On the positive side, maternal mortality is now down 26 percent compared to 1990.[1]

To combat the slow progress in achieving the improvements to maternal and reproductive health set forth by the MDG, a partnership between the United Nations Population Fund and the Millennium Villages Project emerged in late 2010. These large international organizations established plans to work toward universal access to reproductive healthcare by partnering with community groups throughout Africa while also leaning on medical researchers to determine the most efficient and effective ways to medically improve reproductive health. National governments will also be involved in helping to determine the direction of these projects. Through this initiative, we see recognition of the need for donors to work with community programs to truly effect change. Grassroots organizations have better access and greater influence with local women but often work with meager resources. On the other hand, UN initiatives often carry large budgets but have less success in gaining respect and meaningful contact with target audiences. The hope is that money and science will enhance grassroots programs focused on women's health.

Perhaps the biggest challenge for women's reproductive health is gaining support from the African population. Although an increasing number of African women and men do see the need to expand women's health services, there are still many who deem reproductive healthcare unnecessary and wasteful. This may be in part due to miscommunication of what reproductive health actually entails, as many Africans associate it simply with access to abortion and preventing pregnancy through contraceptive use. While it is true that these are features of reproductive health, these are only some of the options afforded by improved women's health services. With maternal and infant mortality rates unsatisfactorily high, in part due to multiple pregnancies without appropriate spacing, it is clear to many healthcare providers that women and babies would be much healthier if women practiced family planning to space and limit pregnancies.

---

[1] Women Deliver. "Maternal and Reproductive Health Issues Take Center Stage in Africa." *Modern Ghana*, March 27, 2012.

It will be largely up to community advocates for women's health to inform local communities of the value of improved women's health-care beyond the more divisive topics of abortion and birth control.

MENTAL HEALTH

In 2012 the World Health Organization reported that untreated mental, neurological, and substance use disorders accounted for more than 13 percent of the global disease burden, which measures the combined years of life lost due to premature mortality and poor health. They estimate that by the year 2030, depression will be the leading cause of disease burden worldwide. Another recent study found that mortality rates from suicide and from physical disease among persons with mental illness were comparable to global mortality rates from HIV/AIDS and malaria. Despite striking evidence confirming the significance of this problem, policymakers have not considered mental health a priority (Jenkins et al., 2010). This is certainly true in sub-Saharan Africa, where 70 percent of governments have routinely allocated less than 1 percent of their annual health budgets to mental health (Bird et al., 2010).

Part of the problem is that mental illness is highly stigmatized. In Uganda, for instance, stigma not only keeps mentally ill people from seeking medical care but also deters health workers from specializing in the field. In a 2008 study by the Mental Health and Poverty Project, one official from the Ugandan Ministry of Health was quoted as saying that medical students in Kampala believed that if they practiced psychiatry, they would eventually develop mental health problems themselves.[2] This fear is evidenced by the fact that there are only thirty-two psychiatrists in the entire country. With a population of more than 34 million people, this means that each psychiatrist carries a potential caseload of more than 1 million patients. As a result of this glaring disparity, more than 65 percent of the mentally ill do not receive psychiatric treatment. In neighboring Kenya, where there are only eighty-three qualified psychiatrists in a nation of 40 million people, the health burden is even greater. According to David M. Ndetei, a professor at the University of Nairobi and the director of the African Mental Health Foundation, only 4 percent of Kenyans with

---

[2] Richard Kavuma. "Changing Perceptions of Mental Health in Uganda." *The Guardian*, May 19, 2010.

mental illness are able to access treatment options.[3] If democratization is about creating spaces for the inclusion of additional voices and interests as Andrea Cornwall and Anne-Marie Goetz (2005) have suggested, then the historical politics of mental illness must be taken seriously.

In order to make up for the dearth of formal psychiatric care, many Ugandans have come to rely upon a broad network of traditional healers. Not only are they widely accessible, but they are also part of a wider cultural belief system that is considered integral to well-being. One recent study, conducted in Jinja and Iganga Districts, found that 60 percent of those who attended healing shrines had moderate to severe mental illness (Abbo et al., 2009). Another study, conducted in Kabarole District and published in 2002, found that 30 percent of households surveyed had at least one member with a mental illness of some sort. Most did not receive treatment because of the lack of services available. In fact, isolation was the primary mechanism of managing mental illness in that particular community, which included tying sufferers to a tree, locking them into a house, or putting them into prison. Because mental illness is often associated with witchcraft or demonic possession, sufferers have also been subject to physical abuse and mob justice. Although the Uganda Witchcraft Act of 1957 outlaws these violent practices, the failure of authorities to take action against so-called witchcraft practitioners has produced frustration and has prompted people "to kill witches and sorcerers, and to rid the community of the peddlers of this evil craft" (Nsereko, 1996, p. 44).

Traditional healing practices have also become increasingly common in South Africa, particularly since the transition to democracy in 1994. In an effort to cleanse the nation of its apartheid past, many South Africans have come to embrace a wide variety of healing methods. Interestingly enough, traditional healers have become a modern way of treating mental illness. Robert Thornton, the head of the Anthropology Department at the University of Witwatersrand, notes that since the mid-1990s, more and more people have become traditional healers, or *sangomas*. These practitioners, just like their clients, come from all racial and ethnic backgrounds. "For many," he says, "*sangomas* appear to preserve a sense of a distinctive 'African' identity in an increasingly globalized and 'Westernized' country"

---

[3] Rodney Muhumuza. "Psychiatrists Decry Mental Health Care in Africa." *The Boston Globe*, July 18, 2013.

(Thornton, 2009, p. 17). Thornton explains that *sangomas* are not necessarily "traditional," nor are they "healers." They are more like teachers and learners. They offer a wide range of counseling, divination, medical, and other services, such as preparing traditional medicines to protect their clients from all sorts of ills. They also relieve anxiety and depression, find lost objects, and help people make decisions. The South African government recognizes the importance of *sangomas* and treats them like medical practitioners. In 2004 they passed the Traditional Health Practitioners Act to regulate their conduct and to standardize their healing practices. This is an important step in helping the nation to heal from a violent past while addressing the significant mental health challenges of the twenty-first century.

CONCLUSION

In an article published in 2005 in *QJM: An International Journal of Medicine*, Jennifer Ruger argues that to better understand the determinants of health and illness, we must look beyond economic measures and explore the linkages between political institutions and global health inequalities. She explains that because democracies are dependent on voter support, "[d]emocratic institutions might therefore relate to health through, for example, alleviation of social disparities and income inequalities that results from greater political voice and participation. . . . Political institutions might also affect health through their general impact on universal health policy issues, such as universal access to high-quality services" (Ruger, 2005, pp. 299–300). On the other hand, she argues, "the absence of representative democracy provides few incentives for political elites to compete for votes, resulting in less political responsiveness and few incentives to spread benefits universally or to the poor. Authoritarian regimes suppress political competition and tend to have an interest in preventing human development, because improved health, education, and economic security mobilizes citizens to advocate for greater participation and more resources" (p. 300). Although we see community-based initiatives to prevent and treat illness, the burden of public health cannot be placed solely on the communities most vulnerable and weakened by health threats. If Ruger is correct in her thesis, democracy, or perhaps more precisely good governance, could positively affect the health and healing of the African population. National budgets must allocate more resources to public health. Although the initial costs would be a difficult burden to shoulder, the long-term payoffs might prove valuable. If African countries were not debilitated by large, unhealthy groups within the population, the peripheral costs of poor health could be alleviated. There is a profound need to support the work of grassroots health organizations while also addressing the larger causes of health crises, and it is hoped that current and future governments throughout Africa will find value in promoting health and healing.

REFERENCES

Abbo, Catherine, et al. "The Prevalence and Severity of Mental Illnesses Handled by Traditional Healers in Two Districts in Uganda." *African Health Sciences* 9, no. 1 (2009): 16–22.

AVERT. http://www.avert.org/history-hiv-aids-africa.htm (accessed September 23, 2013).

Bill & Melinda Gates Foundation. http://www.gatesfoundation.org/What-We-Do/Global-Health/Malaria (accessed September 23, 2013).

Bird, Philippa, et al. "Increasing the Priority of Mental Health in Africa: Findings from Qualitative Research in Ghana, South Africa, Uganda and Zambia." *Health Policy and Planning* 26 (2010): 357–365.

Cooper, Frederick. *Africa since 1940: The Past of the Present.* Cambridge, U.K.: Cambridge University Press, 2002.

Cornwall, Andrea, and Anne-Marie Goetz. "Democratizing Democracy: Feminist Perspectives." *Democratization* 12, no. 5 (2005): 783–800.

Jenkins, R., et al. "Mental Health and the Development Agenda in Sub-Saharan Africa." *Psychiatric Services* 61, no. 3 (March 2010): 229–234.

Nsereko, Daniel D. N. "Witchcraft as a Criminal Defense: From Uganda to Canada and Back." *Manitoba Law Journal* 24 (1996): 38–59.

Roll Back Malaria Partnership. http://www.rollbackmalaria.org/keyfacts.html (accessed September 23, 2013).

Ruger, Jennifer Prah. "Democracy and Health." *QJM: An International Journal of Medicine* 98, no. 4 (2005): 299–304.

TANU. "Tanzania Ten Years After." Dar es Salaam: Government Printer, 1971.

Thornton, Robert. "The Transmission of Knowledge in South Africa Traditional Healing." *Africa* 79, no. 1 (2009): 17–34.

UNAIDS. *Global Report: UNAIDS Report on the Global AIDS Epidemic 2012.* New York: UNAIDS, 2012.

UNICEF. http://www.unicef.org/health/index_malaria.html (accessed September 23, 2013).

WHO. *Global Burden of Mental Disorders and the Need for a Comprehensive, Coordinated Response from Health and Social Sectors at the Country Level.* Geneva: WHO, 2012.

WHO, UNICEF, and UNAIDS. *Progress Report 2011: Global HIV/AIDS Response: Epidemic Update and Health Sector Progress Towards Universal Access.* Geneva: World Health Organization, 2011.

SUGGESTED READINGS/FILMS/WEBSITES

Chirowa, Frank, Stephen Atwood, and Marc Van der Putten. *Gender Inequality: Health Expenditure and Maternal Mortality in Sub-Saharan Africa.* Saarbrücken, Germany: Lambert Academic Publishing, 2012.

Epstein, Helen. *The Invisible Cure: Why We Are Losing the Fight Against AIDS in Africa.* New York: Picador, 2008.

Nolen, Stephanie. *28: Stories of AIDS in Africa.* New York: Walker Publishing Company, 2007.

Roodt, Darrell. *Yesterday,* DVD. HBO Films, 2004.

Steinberg, Jonny. *Sizwe's Test: A Young Man's Journey through Africa's AIDS Epidemic.* New York: Simon & Schuster, 2008.

Vitoria, M., et al. "The Global Fight against HIV/AIDS, Tuberculosis, and Malaria: Current Status and Future Perspectives." *American Journal of Clinical Pathology* 131 (2009): 844–848.

Women, Gender,
and Sexuality

Democratization transformed the larger political landscape by creating new opportunities to debate the politics of women, gender, and sexuality in Africa. These conversations took place in multiple arenas and involved a wide variety of participants, all of whom represented diverse experiences and interests. The United Nations played a key role in facilitating many of these early discussions. After the General Assembly declared 1975 as International Women's Year in recognition of the fact that women throughout the world continued to experience discrimination on a daily basis, they convened the first World Conference on Women in Mexico City with the themes of equality, development, and peace. This meeting was important in that it provided an opportunity for many women's voices to be heard. Women headed 113 official member state delegations (out of 133) but also participated actively in a parallel forum for nongovernmental organizations, which attracted nearly four thousand persons. Two major outcomes were the Declaration of Mexico on the Equality of Women and Their Contribution to Development and Peace, 1975, as well as a World Plan of Action for the Implementation of the Objectives of the International Women's Year. Both served as roadmaps for the global women's movement.

After the conference in Mexico City, the General Assembly declared the period from 1976 until 1985 as the United Nation's Decade for Women, and established a Voluntary Fund to support activities which enabled member states to implement the World Plan of Action. In 1979, they adopted the Convention on the Elimination of All Forms of Discrimination against Women (CEDAW), which became known as an international bill of rights for women. The Convention explicitly defined discrimination against women and established a framework for ending such discrimination. The following year, the UN convened its second World Conference on Women in Copenhagen, which assessed progress made since the first conference and outlined plans for the second half of the Decade. A third conference was held in Nairobi in 1985 to mark the end of the Decade. Not surprisingly, African women played a significant role in the proceedings. The final conference document, the Nairobi Forward-Looking Strategies for the Advancement of Women, reflected their contributions to the deliberations and charted a path for achieving the objectives outlined in previous conference resolutions by the year 2000. A fourth (and thus far) final conference was held in Beijing in 1995 and resulted in a Declaration and Platform for Action, which identified twelve critical areas of concern. These areas continue to form the basis for all UN activities and interventions organized on behalf of the world's women.

These United Nations conferences provided African women with a forum in which they could debate the issues that were most central to their lives. Their voices were also heard, or at least represented, at the regional level. In 1977, the UN Economic Commission for Africa began organizing a series of smaller conferences that focused exclusively on African women. The first Regional Conference on the Integration of Women in Development was held in Nouakchott, Mauritania, to review progress made by member states and nongovernmental organizations in implementing the Regional Plan of Action, which was adopted at the World Conference on Women in Mexico City in 1975. In 1979 they met in Lusaka, Zambia, to review progress and prepare for the second World Conference on Women in Copenhagen. It was another five years before a third Regional Conference on Women was held, this time in Arusha, Tanzania. Participants once again reviewed the progress they had made and examined the obstacles they had encountered in attaining their goals for women's advancement. They also formulated a position paper in preparation for the World Conference on Women in Nairobi titled, "Arusha Strategies for the Advancement of Women in Africa: Beyond the End of the United Nations Decade for Women." Although the United Nations did not organize another World Conference on Women in 1990, the Economic Commission for Africa convened a fourth Regional Conference on Women, which was held in Abuja, Nigeria, in 1989. Widely attended by heads of state, observers from the UN and various nongovernmental organizations, as well as African women from all walks of life, this conference positioned women as key development planners and actors, not as passive recipients of aid. At the opening ceremony, Suzanne Mubarak, then first lady of Egypt, offered her vision for development:

> I have faith and confidence in the people of Africa, in the intelligence of mankind and, above all, in the wisdom and integrity of African women. I genuinely believe that the problems of our continent, be they social, economic or political, can be solved by Africans alone. Africa is blessed by its human resources, its natural resources and by the economic and social potential yet untapped. Let us, therefore, combine our efforts and stand united in spite of the problems confronting us. (Mubarak, 1989, p. 4)

Mubarak recognized that African challenges could only be solved through African solutions, an important theme that continued to emerge in the years to come. The final conference document, the Abuja Declaration on Participatory Development, specifically outlined the role of African women in this process. These ideas were further developed and refined at additional regional conferences, which took place in Dakar, Senegal (1994), Addis Ababa, Ethiopia (1999 and 2004), and Banjul, Gambia (2009). The declarations and action plans that came out of these meetings are valuable primary source documents because they reveal the centrality of women to African development over the last three decades. For ease of reference, they are listed as recommended readings at the end of this chapter.

The African Union has also taken up a leadership role in advancing women's rights on the continent. The promotion of gender equity is enshrined in Article 4 of the governing body's Constitutive Act. At their second summit, held in Maputo, Mozambique, in 2003, they adopted the Protocol to the African Charter on Human and People's Rights on the Rights of Women in Africa, discussed in greater detail later in the chapter. This important Protocol went into effect in late 2005 after it was ratified by the requisite fifteen governments. At their third summit, held in Addis Ababa in 2004, they endorsed another important instrument for promoting gender equality and women's empowerment—the Solemn Declaration on Gender Equality in Africa. As part of this Declaration, African leaders agreed to report their country's progress toward gender equality on an annual basis. The Chair of the AU Commission was also expected to submit an annual report to the Assembly of Heads of State and Government on progress made in implementing the Solemn Declaration as well as on the state of gender equality and gender mainstreaming at the national and regional levels.

In order to assist member states with their reporting duties, the Ministers Responsible for Women's Affairs and Gender adopted two key documents at their first ministerial summit held in Dakar in 2005, namely the Implementation Framework for the Solemn Declaration on Gender Equality in Africa (SDGEA) and the Guidelines for Monitoring and Reporting on the SDGEA. At their second summit, held in Maseru, Lesotho, in 2008, they called on the African Union to declare 2010–2020 as African Women's Decade. Shortly thereafter, the Assembly adopted the ministers' proposal. Under the auspices of the Directorate of Women, Gender, and Development, the ministers organized three additional summits to promote the advancement of African women: Banjul (2009) and Addis Ababa (2011 and 2013). They also played a key role in helping to create the African Union Gender Policy, which was formally adopted in 2009.

African governments have also played an important role in promoting women's rights and gender equality, which in turn has created opportunities for the voices of the marginalized to be heard and their needs recognized. Many have enacted legislation at national and local levels to protect women from various forms of discrimination. Apart from South Africa, however, most countries have not passed laws that offer protection on the basis of gender identity or sexual orientation, a significant problem that we address below. In addition to legal frameworks, most African states have also developed formal institutions to advance the status of women, known generally as "national machineries." These include women's bureaus, ministries, policies, plans, and programs to integrate women into national development. Although national machineries helped to democratize or open up political space, states also stifled or co-opted democratic impulses. Throughout the 1980s, for instance, many African governments required women's groups to operate under a larger umbrella organization, which was frequently attached to the ruling party. These de facto "women's wings" were supposed to cater to women's affairs, but in reality they simply channeled women into state patronage networks. In many cases, women's groups were placed under the control of the first lady or another female relative of a party leader. By the 1990s, however, most organizations had disentangled themselves from the state and were able to select their own leaders, frame their own agendas, and fund their own initiatives (Tripp et al., 2009).

Autonomous women's organizations were central actors within African democratization processes, not only because they brought marginalized voices to the proverbial table but also because they were able to clearly demonstrate why those voices mattered. The One Million Signatures Campaign in Morocco is an excellent case in point. In 1992, the Women's Action Union circulated a petition that called for the reform of the *Mudawana*, or family laws that determined the personal legal status of men, women, and children and the relationships among them. The laws were promulgated shortly after independence and based on a very narrow interpretation of Islamic jurisprudence, which was harmful to women's rights. Although the laws were no longer relevant to modern society, many were afraid to debate or change them because of their "sacredness." By crafting a petition calling for reform and then sending that petition to the media, the parliament, and even the king, the women made the personal political. They wrote:

> We, the undersigned, declare that we strongly believe that only a democratization of relations within the family and society in general can lead to the construction of a real democracy. The Personal Status Law articles are in utter contradiction to the Moroccan Constitution, which explicitly guarantees equality between men and women. The present Personal Status Law is out of date and its articles are unjust toward women, as they cause unnecessary family crises and social strategies. We, here, demand to change its articles according to the following principles. . . . (Women's Action Union, 1992, p. 278)

The petition inspired great public debate, and citizens began to realize that the *Mudawana* could be changed. As Fatima Bouabdelli writes, "Gathering one million signatures for any reason in a developing Muslim country like Morocco was an accomplishment; gathering them for the cause of women's rights was a spectacular feat" (Bouabdelli, 2009, p. 277). The petition faced tremendous resistance from the Minister of Islamic Affairs and from religious authorities. Local imams even circulated a counterpetition opposing any change to the *Mudawana* and declared a *fatwa*, or religious edict, criminalizing the women's group and threatening its members with death. Such actions, however, only served to further politicize the petition. The petition compelled the government to change key articles of the laws, which ultimately paved the way for more significant reforms in 2003. Women's organizing was indeed an important force for democratization.

In the rest of this chapter we examine four case studies that examine how African women's activism has facilitated the democratization of formal politics as well as other types of political space. We also consider the extent to which democratization has (or has not) facilitated dialogues about larger political issues that have a bearing on women, gender, and sexuality in Africa. In the first section we discuss the evolution of the Maputo Protocol, paying particular attention to African women's role in pushing for its adoption in various political arenas. The next section analyzes the emergence of academic feminism and how this led to a democratization of the African academy. In the third section we explore the controversial debates surrounding female genital cutting and question whether political democratization has, in fact, created the space for Africans to discuss the complexities of this issue. Finally, in the last section we look at the gay rights movement as an illustration of the limitations of democratization. We maintain that political liberalization has not created a safe space for sexual minorities in most parts of Africa today.

THE AFRICAN CHARTER ON WOMEN'S RIGHTS

The African Charter on Human and Peoples' Rights on the Rights of Women in Africa, or the Maputo Protocol, grew out of a growing recognition that women were marginalized within the political, economic, and social landscapes of postcolonial Africa. Women were not integrated into the power structures that dictated policies and dominated commerce, and women's unique interests and concerns were pushed to the periphery of national agendas and discourse. Simply put, women in postcolonial Africa were silenced by structural and cultural systems of male privilege and therefore were not a part of the political democratization process. It is for this reason that African feminists began intensifying their efforts to generate attention for women's rights and concerns.

In 1990, following a women's empowerment conference held in Harare, Zimbabwe, a group of feminist activists created Women in

Law and Development in Africa (WiLDAF). This important organization, which is now comprised of representatives from thirty-one countries and has over five hundred organizations included in its network, was instrumental in garnering international attention and support for African women's rights. In 1995 they held a meeting in Lome, Togo, where participants appealed for the development of a protocol that integrated women's rights into the African Charter on Human and Peoples' Rights. That charter, adopted in June 1981 by the Organization of African Unity (OAU), had effectively neutralized gender by implying that women and men understand and experience rights and violations in the same way. One Nigerian law professor argues that by not explicitly addressing women's rights, women continue to be subjected to a "hidden male bias in this model" and "[a]ccording to this 'sameness' model, women (who do not conform to the male standard) are denied the fruits of equality. In emphasising the sameness of women and men, gender specificity and the 'woman's issue' are erased" (Aniekwu, 2009, p. 24). In other words, the African Charter on Human and Peoples' Rights reified male privilege and obscured the particular rights that offered women security and stability.

WiLDAF and its supporters argued that the African Charter on Human and Peoples' Rights failed to address the specific needs of African women and fell short in providing protection of women's rights. The push to incorporate a women's rights addendum began at the Lome conference in 1995 and came to fruition in 2003 when the African Union (AU) met in Maputo, Mozambique, and approved the Protocol to the African Charter on Human and Peoples' Rights on the Rights of Women in Africa. This protocol included articles that addressed the elimination of discrimination against women, the elimination of harmful practices, equal status in marriage, the right to separate, divorce, and/or annul marriages, the right to participate in political and decision-making processes, protection of women in armed conflicts, the right to education and training, economic and social welfare rights, health and reproductive rights, rights to food security, adequate housing, positive cultural context, healthy and sustainable environments, inheritance rights, and special protection of elderly women. By adopting this important piece of international legislation, member states of the AU are expected to strive toward achieving and maintaining women's rights as promised in the Protocol. Many of these rights have not been consistently accessible or realized, so African women have been forced to continue the fight.

FIGURE 4.1   The Maputo Protocol was instrumental in garnering international attention and support for women's rights. In some countries, such as Uganda, it is common to see women's leadership promoted on everything from billboards to bumper stickers and tire covers. Photograph by Adrianna Ernstberger, 2011.

ACADEMIC FEMINISM

African women have played an important role in democratizing many different kinds of political space, not least of which is within the academy. Since the late 1970s and early 80s, they have established feminist scholarly networks that have brought new voices and ideas to the proverbial table, thus challenging the ways in which knowledge is produced and disseminated across the disciplines. One of the first such organizations was the Association of African Women for Research and Development, which was established in Dakar, Senegal, in 1977 to promote the economic, political, and social rights of African women through various research, training, and advocacy projects. It has played a key role in educating African governments about gender issues and helping them to better understand why women's contributions to development should be taken seriously. Unfortunately, like many other nongovernmental organizations in the Global South, the Association has faced a number of challenges in recent years, including a lack of sustained funding, which has significantly reduced its ability to conduct research and promote change on local, regional, and global levels.

Another important feminist network that got its start around this time was the Women's Research and Documentation Project, which brought Tanzanian women together to informally discuss "the woman question." Two years later, in 1980, the women became formally affiliated with the Institute of Development Studies at the University of Dar es Salaam. Within a short period of time, however, members decided to sever their ties with the Institute after running into trouble with male leaders over control of resources and policy making. The women did not want the fruits of their labor to be expropriated and chose to go off on their own. When they formally established the Project in 1983, they articulated several broad goals. These were:

> to promote the critical study and research of the women's question and gender issues in Tanzania in relation to problems and strategies of development at the local, national, and international levels; to focus on analysis of women in Africa in the context of issues of decolonization, national liberation, and socialist transformation; to use research, documentation, writing and publications, and seminars to develop broad-based communications about gender issues and the women's question among Tanzanian women in particular; to develop a supportive context and collective framework for members and others who are concerned about women's issues; and to promote and encourage a participatory approach in research. (Meena and Mbilinyi, 1991, p. 852)

This organization served as a model for similar projects that emerged throughout the continent in later years. In Nigeria, for instance, a group of female academics established the Women's Research and Documentation Center at the University of Ibadan in late 1986. Similar to their Tanzanian colleagues, they sought to conduct research, organize seminars, promote policy, and provide links to other women's research and policy centers throughout Africa and beyond. These types of initiatives were important because they privileged women's experiences and analyses, something that had been missing in most academic scholarship until this point.

Democratization of the academy was not just about research but also teaching. In 1979, Ahmadu Bello University in Nigeria offered its first women's studies course through the Sociology Department. Although this was an important milestone, it would take nearly a decade for women's studies to be considered an academic discipline in its own right. In 1988 the Center of African Studies at Eduardo Mondlane University in Mozambique created a Women's Studies Department. In addition to producing scholarship on women in Mozambique, they trained gender specialists, maintained a library on feminist issues, and collaborated with state and nonstate organizations on various projects. The following year, similar programs were established at the University of Ghana, Ahfad University in Sudan, and the University of Pretoria in South Africa.

One of the most prominent programs is located within the School of Women and Gender Studies at Makerere University in Uganda. After attending the Nairobi conference in 1985, a group of scholars and activists got together to form Action for Development (ACFODE), a nongovernmental organization that sought to empower Ugandan women both within and outside of the academy. In July 1987 representatives from ACFODE and the Uganda Association of University Women presented a paper to the University's Donor Conference in which they called for the creation of a women's studies program within the Faculty of Social Sciences. Support for their proposal was overwhelming, and soon a committee was formed to formulate structure and content. The University Council formally approved the program in October 1989, and two years later the Department of Women's Studies became fully operational. They began offering a two-year master's degree course as well as short-term evening courses for local decision-makers and development practitioners. In 1999 they introduced a three-year undergraduate course as well as a Ph.D. training program. The Department gained international recognition when they hosted the Women's Worlds Conference in 2002. They achieved even greater prominence in 2011 when they became the first School of Women and Gender Studies on the continent, replete with their own dean.

Another program that has made significant contributions to the democratization of the academy is the African Gender Institute at the

University of Cape Town in South Africa, which was established in 1996 in order to "provide a safe space where women in the academy could develop their intellectual and leadership capacities; where African women writers, researchers, policy-makers and practitioners would be given new opportunities; [and] where Africa-centric applied knowledges of gender, transformation, and democratic practice could be developed and propagated" (African Gender Institute, 2013). The Institute became a formal organizational unit within the university in 1999 and began offering undergraduate and graduate degrees in gender and women's studies. They have also designed and implemented projects

FIGURE 4.2   In many parts of Africa, men are strong advocates of women's empowerment. This Ugandan man wears a "Stop Violence Against Women" shirt to demonstrate his support for domestic violence prevention work in Kampala. Photograph by Alicia C. Decker, 2012.

that enhance research, networking, capacity building, and knowledge creation throughout the continent. Since 2002 they have been publishing a peer-reviewed scholarly journal called *Feminist Africa*, which has succeeded in bringing African women's knowledge and experiences to the fore. Their work, like that of many of their feminist colleagues, has opened up exciting new political spaces for women (and men) across Africa.

FEMALE GENITAL CUTTING

The prevalence of female genital cutting (FGC) in Africa draws much attention to issues of women's rights and women's health as various internal and external groups consider the moral and legal validity of the practice. But to what extent has democratization created the space for Africans to discuss the complexities of this issue? Many African women would argue that their voices are still silenced within global debates about this controversial feminist topic, regardless of where they stand on the issue. Donor governments and/or international organizations often see them as "target populations" for their interventions but not as development partners or change agents in their own right. Democratization may provide opportunities for more people to sit at the table, but as this case study demonstrates, this does not mean that everyone will be able to speak or be heard.

FGC, also referred to as female genital mutilation and female circumcision, is widely practiced throughout Africa and usually takes one of four forms. Clitoridectomy is the partial or complete removal of the clitoris. Excision involves the removal of the clitoris and labia minora and sometimes includes removal of the labia majora. The more invasive form of FGC, infibulation, is the removal of the clitoris as well as other parts of the external genitalia, such as the labia minora and labia majora. Typically infibulation is completed by sewing the remaining sides of the labia majora together with only a small hole left to allow for urination and menstruation. A fourth category involves other variations of operations on female genitalia, such as piercings and incisions, cauterizations, scraping and cutting, and the application of corrosive liquids or herbs.

Communities that practice FGC consider it an important rite of passage and believe that their cultural and/or religious traditions justify the procedure. Proponents of the practice argue that it will minimize promiscuity and protect women's virginity. Although all forms of FGC are painful and often conducted in unhygienic settings, infibulation is particularly dangerous. Women are susceptible to hemorrhaging during the procedure, tetanus and other infections at the site if healing does not occur, organ damage, urethra swelling, and blockage. It can also cause chronic pelvic infections, infertility, abscesses and scar tissue, intense pain and tearing during intercourse, and it threatens the lives of fetuses and pregnant women during childbirth. Women who are cut are also more vulnerable to HIV. Many girls and women who experience the practice also develop psychological conditions such as shock, trauma, anxiety, and depression.

Numerous women's rights groups and public health organizations within and outside of Africa see FGC as one of the continent's most pressing violations against the rights of girls and women. The World Health Organization (WHO) estimates that in Africa, 101 million girls aged ten and older have experienced FGC and that every year over 3 million girls are at risk of having FGC performed on them. In the late 1990s local and international efforts to eradicate the practice intensified after WHO identified FGC as a pressing health concern. During the first decade of the twenty-first century, they widely publicized FGC and its detrimental health consequences in the hopes of eradicating the practice. The UN General Assembly recently joined the international lobby by unanimously adopting a resolution calling for the elimination of the practice. According to a UN Women's summary, the "resolution urges countries to condemn all harmful practices that affect women and girls, in particular female genital mutilations, and to take all necessary measures, including enforcing legislation, awareness-raising and allocating sufficient resources to protect women and girls from this form of violence. It calls for special attention to protect women and girls who have been subjected to female genital mutilations, and those at risk, including refugee women and women migrants" (UN Women, 2012). The position of the international community strongly favors the eradication of FGC as a means of protecting the bodies and rights of girls and women.

Despite the general consensus among outsiders on the topic, FGC is much more controversial within Africa and the Middle East, where it mainly occurs. African communities, politicians, and FGC proponents and opponents are split on how to define FGC, with some arguing that it is a cultural and/or religious rite of passage, while others declare it a violation of human and women's rights as well as a public health threat. African women are divided on the issue as well.

Advocates pushing for the eradication of FGC include African celebrities like Senegalese hip-hop artist Sister Fa, who publicly announced that she had undergone FGC and urges fellow Senegalese to join her in the push to end the practice. Likewise, political figures such as the first ladies of Burkina Faso and Benin also joined the campaign to end the practice. Support to stop FGC also comes from grassroots women's groups, such as Somalia's Mudug Women's Development Network and Kenya's Rural Women Peace Link, both of which educate about the dangers of FGC. New grassroots organizations are created every year throughout Africa with the goal of using African women and men to educate fellow citizens about the dangers of the practice. Many believe that tangible change will only occur when average women and men convince their own communities to drop the practice.

On the other side of the debate are African community leaders, FGC practitioners, scholars, and women who have undergone FGC and who believe it is an important practice to continue. Fuambai Ahmadu, a Sierra Leonean feminist scholar, argues that the involvement of outsiders in discussions about FGC drowns out the voices of millions of African women who are not offended by the practice and who consider it an important personal choice they should be allowed to make. She also challenges the notion that FGC necessarily results in serious health risks. In one interview Ahmadu pointed out that "most women do not experience it as mutilation and would never refer to themselves as mutilated" and that for many women, herself included, "there was absolutely no difference in terms of . . . sexual experience, sexual feeling, [or] ability to achieve orgasm."[1] Although proponents of FGC face increasing criticism, many African women continue to believe that they cannot be "true" women without the procedure. Critics of the practice, however, return to the fact that the procedure is usually conducted on girls who are not fully aware of the potential harms or who do not know that they have the right to choose for themselves what is and is not done to their bodies. FGC will continue to be a polarizing point of contention in the years to come, but African women must be given the opportunity to take the lead and frame the debate in ways that are most empowering to them. This is, after all, the point of democratization.

---

[1] "Circumcised Women Can Have Healthy Sex Lives: Expert." *World News Australia*, February 19, 2013.

GAY RIGHTS

Democratization has thus far opened up very little political space for sexual minorities in Africa. Members of the lesbian, gay, bisexual, transgender, and queer (LGBTQ) communities have experienced substantial hostility, discrimination, and violence as a result of their sexual identity or orientation. More than two-thirds of all African countries currently have laws criminalizing consensual same-sex acts.

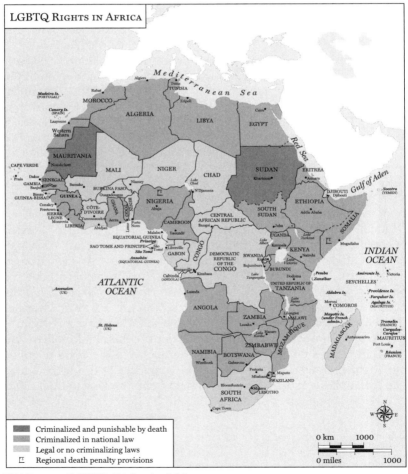

MAP 4.1 LGBTQ Rights in Africa

In Uganda, Tanzania, and Sierra Leone, for instance, offenders face life imprisonment for engaging in homosexual acts. In Mauritania, Sudan, northern Nigeria, and parts of southern Somalia, homosexuality is punishable by death. Although same-sex sexual activity is legal in nineteen African countries and legal *for women only* in five others, South Africa is the only one that provides full rights and legal protections to sexual minorities. The "equality clause" within the Bill of Rights provides all citizens with the right to equal protection under the law, regardless of gender, sex, or sexual orientation. When parliamentarians passed the Civil Union Act in December 2006, South Africa became the first (and only) country on the continent to legalize gay marriage.

South Africa has a long history of gay rights activism. Although homosexuality was a crime that was punishable by up to seven years in prison throughout the apartheid era, a number of LGBTQ groups formed in the late 1970s. Most, however, remained divided along racial lines. The Gay Association of South Africa, for instance, was established in Johannesburg in 1982 and focused primarily on the needs of white men. They disbanded in 1986 over political differences, since some members wanted to support the liberation struggle while others remained loyal to the white National Party. Two years later a group of activists tried to bridge the racial divide by forming GLOW, the Gay and Lesbian Organization of the Witwatersrand. They organized the country's first Pride march in October 1990. At this momentous event, Simon Nkoli, one of the group's leaders, made the statement, "In South Africa I am oppressed because I am a black man, and I am oppressed because I am gay. So when I fight for my freedom I must fight against both oppressions." He continued the fight until his untimely death in 1998, another tragic victim of the AIDS pandemic.

The National Coalition for Gay and Lesbian Equality was another important historical actor in the struggle for gay rights in South Africa. Established in December 1994, this group coordinated many local LGBTQ organizations and successfully lobbied for the inclusion of sexual orientation as a basis for nondiscrimination laws in the country after the end of apartheid. One of their allies was Archbishop Desmond Tutu, who submitted the following letter of support to the Constitutional Assembly of the South African Parliament on June 2, 1995:

Within the Church of Christ, and indeed amongst adherents of other faiths, there is much debate and difference of opinion on the question of homosexuality. The theological and ethical issues are complex and far from resolved. It is indisputable, however, that people's sexual nature is fundamental to their humanity. The apartheid regime enacted laws upon the religious convictions of a minority of the country's population, laws which denied gay and lesbian people their basic human rights and reduced them to social outcasts and criminals in their land of birth. These laws are still on the Statute Books awaiting your decision whether or not to include gay and lesbian people in the "Rainbow People" of South Africa. It would be a sad day for South Africa if any individual or group of law-abiding citizens in South Africa were to find that the Final Constitution did not guarantee their fundamental human right to a sexual life, whether heterosexual or homosexual. I would strongly urge you to include the sexual orientation clause in the Final Constitution.

In December 1996, President Nelson Mandela enacted the new constitution with the equality clause intact. Although gay rights are now firmly protected by the law, members of the LGBTQ community have experienced a significant backlash in recent years. So-called corrective rapes against lesbians have become increasingly common, as have other types of violent hate crimes, clear evidence that democratization has not been a panacea for social injustice.

No country has earned more notoriety because of its harsh anti-gay climate than Uganda. Although anti-sodomy laws have been on the books for more than sixty years, most citizens were not concerned about homosexuality until the media introduced it as a subject of national debate. On August 8, 2006, *The Red Pepper*, one of the country's leading tabloids, published the names and detailed descriptions of forty-five men whom they claimed were gay or bisexual. They also provided a phone number for readers to report other alleged homosexuals. One month later, they published a similar defamatory article targeting local lesbians. The paper fanned the flames of hatred by publishing additional lists of suspected homosexuals over the coming months. The media were not alone in promoting homophobia. In September 2009 three prominent American evangelicals spoke at a large religious revival in Kampala. They discussed how to make gay people straight, how gay men "recruited" teen boys into the "lifestyle," and how the gay movement wanted to defeat marriage and replace it with a culture of sexual promiscuity. Local religious leaders also played a key role by spreading hatred and fear among their congregants.

The most disturbing articulation of these homophobic sentiments came in October 2009 when a conservative politician, David Bahati, introduced the infamous Anti-Homosexuality Bill into Parliament. In the name of protecting the "traditional family," the Bill prohibits any form of sexual activity between persons of the same sex and criminalizes the promotion or recognition of these types of sexual relationships. Those convicted of homosexuality would be subject to life imprisonment. If the offender happened to meet any number of additional conditions, known ominously as "aggravated homosexuality," this person could face the death penalty. The Bill also introduces the crime of "failure to disclose the offense," which requires any person in authority to report suspected homosexuals to the relevant authorities within twenty-four hours of acquiring knowledge of an individual's sexual orientation or face three years in prison. This clause simply exacerbates the climate of fear that currently exists in Uganda, turning all citizens into spies for the government. Although the Bill is still pending, its introduction into Parliament has unleashed a flurry of homophobic violence, something that is likely to continue regardless of whether it is eventually passed into law. Clearly, there is still a long way to go before the democratization of the private sphere is fully realized.

CONCLUSION

In 2010 the AU launched with great fanfare the "African Women's Decade." The goal was to stimulate conversations about women's rights and to celebrate women's potential on a grand scale. But this was not the first time that African women were boldly promised a decade devoted to improving the position of women throughout the continent. In 1975, shortly after the first World Conference on Women, the UN declared the commencement of the Women's Decade. During that ten-year period there was much talk about women's rights in Africa, but clearly it was only the beginning of a push for gender equality. By 2010 it was obvious that a lot more work needed to be done to fulfill the promises made to African women regarding their rights and status in their countries and communities. The questions and doubts raised by the failure of the first Women's Decade to bring definitive change continue to plague the new African Women's Decade. Can top-down approaches, often influenced by Global North values and feminisms, really be applied to African women, and is it desirable to use definitions and standards set by outsiders? How loud are the voices of average African women in the discussions about policies geared toward improving their position in society? Even as democratization holds the promise of allowing more women to voice their opinions, it also opens up the possibility for critique of the Global North's imposition of its own values and creates tensions among African populations who of course offer multiple and often oppositional visions of what women's rights and gender equality entails. It remains to be seen the extent to which the AU's African Women's Decade is able to effect positive and widespread change throughout the continent.

REFERENCES

African Gender Institute. "History. University of Cape Town." http://agi.ac.za/about/history (accessed June 14, 2013).

Aniekwu, Nkolika Ijeoma. "The Additional Protocol to the African Charter on Human and People's Rights: Indications of Capacity for African Municipal Systems." *Law, Democracy and Development* 13, no. 2 (2009): 22–35.

Ankrah, E. Maxine, and Peninah D. Bizimana. "Women's Studies Program for Uganda." *Signs: Journal of Women in Culture and Society* 16, no. 4 (Summer 1991): 864–869.

Awe, Bolanle, and Nina Mba. "Women's Research and Documentation Center (Nigeria)." *Signs: Journal of Women in Culture and Society* 16, no. 4 (Summer 1991): 859–864.

Bouabdelli, Fatima. "Latifa Jbabdi and *L'Union de L'Action Féminine*: One Million Signatures." In *Women Writing Africa: The Northern Region*, edited by Fatima Sadiqi et al., pp. 277–278. New York: The Feminist Press at the City University of New York, 2009.

Meena, Ruth, and Marjorie Mbilinyi. "Women's Research and Documentation Project (Tanzania)." *Signs: Journal of Women in Culture and Society* 16, no. 4 (Summer 1991): 852–859.

Mubarak, Suzanne. *Conference Proceedings from the 4th Regional Conference on Women, Abuja, Nigeria, November 6–10, 1989.* http://repository.uneca.org/bitstream/handle/10855/5680/Bib-44867.pdf?sequence=1 (accessed June 21, 2013).

Republic of Uganda. *The Anti-Homosexuality Bill.* 2009.

Tripp, Aili Mari, et al. *African Women's Movements: Changing Political Landscapes.* Cambridge, U.K.: Cambridge University Press, 2009.

Tutu, Archbishop Desmond. "Letter to the South African Constitutional Assembly." June 2, 1995. In *Sex and Politics in South Africa*, edited by Neville

Hoad, Karen Martin, and Graeme Reid, p. 222. Cape Town, South Africa: Juta and Company Limited, 2005.

UN Women. "United Nations bans female genital mutilation." Press release. December 20, 2012. http://www.unwomen.org/2012/12/united-nations-bans-female-genital-mutilation/ (accessed July 6, 2013).

Women's Action Union. "One Million Signatures Petition (1992)." Translated by Fatima Bouabdelli and Fatima Sadiqi. In *Women Writing Africa: The Northern Region*, edited by Fatima Sadiqi et al., p. 278. New York: The Feminist Press at the City University of New York, 2009.

SUGGESTED READINGS/FILMS/WEBSITES

African Union. *Protocol to the African Charter on Human and People's Rights on the Rights of Women in Africa*. Addis Ababa, Ethiopia, 2003.

———. *Solemn Declaration on Gender Equality in Africa*. Addis Ababa, Ethiopia, 2004.

———. *African Union Gender Policy*. Addis Ababa, Ethiopia, 2009.

Bakker, Jacqueline. *The Angel Returns*, DVD. Filmakers Library, 2002.

Berger, Iris, and E. Francis White. *Women in Sub-Saharan Africa: Restoring Women to History*. Bloomington: Indiana University Press, 1999.

Korn, Fadumo. *Born in the Big Rains: A Memoir of Somalia and Survival*. New York: The Feminist Press at the City University of New York, 2004.

Oyěwùmí, Oyèrónké. *The Invention of Women: Making an African Sense of Western Gender Discourses*. Minneapolis: University of Minnesota Press, 1997.

United Nations Economic Commission for Africa. *Report of the Second Regional Conference on the Integration of Women in Development*. Lusaka, Zambia, 1979.

———. *Arusha Strategies for the Advancement of Women in Africa: Beyond the End of the United Nations Decade for Women*. Arusha, Tanzania, 1984.

———. *Abuja Declaration on Participatory Development: The Role of Women in Africa in the 1990s*. Abuja, Nigeria, 1989.

———. *African Platform for Action*. Dakar, Senegal, 1994.

———. *African Plan of Action to Accelerate the Implementation of the Dakar and Beijing Platforms for Action for the Advancement of Women*. Addis Ababa, Ethiopia, 1999.

———. *Decade Review of the Implementation of the Dakar and Beijing Platforms for Action: Outcome and the Way Forward*. Addis Ababa, Ethiopia, 2004.

————. *Banjul Declaration on the Strategies for Accelerating the Implementation of the Dakar and Beijing Platforms for Action: From Commitment to Action*. Banjul, Gambia, 2009.

Wright, Katherine. *Call Me Kuchu*, DVD. Cinedigm Entertainment Group, 2012.

Security

On November 15, 2001, the U.S. Congressional Sub-Committee on Africa convened a hearing on "Africa and the War on Global Terror." Dr. Susan Rice, former assistant secretary of state, testified before the committee about terrorism and its supposed threat to African security. She explained:

> Africa is unfortunately the world's soft underbelly for global terrorism. Al-Qaeda and other terrorist cells are active throughout East, Southern, and West Africa, not to mention North Africa. These organizations hide throughout Africa. They plan, finance, train for, and execute terrorist operations in many parts of Africa, not just from Sudan and Somalia. Terrorist organizations take advantage of Africa's porous borders, weak law enforcement and security services, and nascent judicial institutions to move men, weapons, and money around the globe. They also take advantage of poor, disillusioned populations, often with religious or ethnic grievances, to recruit for their jihad against the civilized world. In short, terrorist networks are exploiting Africa thoroughly. (Rice, 2001)

This statement is problematic for a number of reasons, not least of which is the implication that terrorist networks are to blame for much of Africa's insecurity and exploitation. In actual fact, terrorism represents a relatively minor security threat. The more significant threat is that the vast majority of African states are not able (or willing) to provide for the basic needs of their people. According to the most recent Failed States Index, an empirically-based ranking system that measures a country's risk of failure on the basis of twelve social, economic, and political indicators, African nations are the world's most insecure. In 2013, the five countries with the highest risk of state collapse were

MAP 5.1   Africa and the Failed States Index (2013)

Somalia, Democratic Republic of the Congo, Sudan, South Sudan, and Chad (Fund for Peace, 2013). Given that fifteen of the twenty countries at highest risk are located in Africa, we can surmise that the state poses a more significant threat to security, not global terrorism.

When the African Leadership Forum created the Kampala Document in May 1991, they recognized that democratization was a prerequisite for security, stability, development, and cooperation on the continent. Since that time, however, security has been divorced from larger issues of governance. According to Don Clifton, the dominant approach to security is now the "national security approach," which sees "the unit of focus and the dominant actor as the nation-state, with emphasis on the military as the means by which national security is achieved" (2009, pp. 5–6). The idea is that by securing the nation, citizens will also experience greater security. Unfortunately, there is significant evidence to suggest that militarism does not promote national security but instead increases insecurity, particularly for women (Clarke, 2008; Mama and Okazawa-Rey, 2012). As Claude Ake convincingly argues, "The real security need for Africans is not military security but social security, security against poverty, ignorance, anxiety and fear, disease and famine, against arbitrary power and exploitation, against those things which render democracy improbable in Africa" (2000, p. 147).

In order to promote human security, African leaders need to focus their attention on good governance and sustainable development. Nowhere is this more critical than the urban centers, which are home to nearly 40 percent of the continent's 1 billion people. Southern Africa is the most urbanized region with an average urban population of 58.9 percent, followed by North Africa (51.5 percent), West Africa (44.9 percent), and Central Africa (41.5 percent). The least urbanized region is East Africa, with only 23.7 percent of the population living in urban areas (United Nations Population Division, 2012). Not only are more people living in cities, but the cities themselves are becoming larger and more numerous. There are now forty-three cities in Africa with populations exceeding 1 million inhabitants. Cairo and Lagos both have more than 10 million residents, which classify them as megacities. Because of this rapid population growth, many urban areas have developed large slums and shanty towns. Political scientist Paul D. Williams argues that these slums are "the very epitome of urbanized insecurity, with their residents generally lacking law enforcement, regular sources of employment, sanitation, water, electricity and health-care facilities" (2007, p. 1026). As of 2011, only 42 percent of urbanites in sub-Saharan Africa had access to improved sanitation facilities, or hygienic toilets, compared to 94 percent of urban North Africans (WHO/UNICEF, 2013). The same study found that 84 percent of city dwellers in sub-Saharan Africa had access to clean water, as did 95 percent of those in North African cities. The lack of access to sanitation facilities, together with an inadequate availability of water for hygiene and drinking, has resulted in 88 percent of global diarrheal deaths. When one considers that diarrhea is the leading cause of illness and death worldwide, it becomes easy to see why water and sanitation are such critical security issues within Africa.

Control over natural resources is another significant security issue that is also inextricably linked to good governance and sustainable development. Throughout this book we have seen a number of examples of African states that have erupted into violence as a result of struggles over valuable resources. Sudan was torn apart, quite literally, by the politics of oil. Liberia and Sierra Leone descended into chaos because of diamonds. But in the collapsed state of Somalia, where lawlessness has reigned supreme since President Siad Barre fled the country in 1991, much of the terror and bloodshed has been about fish. Once the government collapsed, it became impossible to enforce the country's fishing rights. Large vessels from dozens of different countries began poaching hundreds of millions of dollars worth of tuna, shrimp, and lobster from the rich waters off the coast (Gilbert and Reynolds, 2012). The Somali fishermen felt they had no choice but to take up arms and seize the other boats. It did not take long before some of them realized that they could earn more money from piracy than they could from fishing. Backed by local militia and international financiers, they began expanding their operations deeper into the Indian Ocean. In 2008, they attracted international attention when they began intercepting ships that were hundreds of miles beyond Somalia's coastal waters. The pirates used small arms and rocket-propelled grenades to threaten the ships. Once they forced their way onboard, they would divert the vessel to a Somali port, often within the semi-autonomous region of Puntland, where they held the ship and its crew hostage until a ransom was paid. While piracy brought in $100 million in revenue in 2009, poaching netted nearly $300 million. Both activities are illegal and have promoted insecurity on a number of different levels, but as historians Eric Gilbert and Jonathan T. Reynolds (2012) rightly note, fish poaching is just not as "exciting" as piracy and therefore receives very little attention.

Not surprisingly, the collapse of the state has created tremendous security challenges for the Somali people as well as for the larger international community. Although threats of piracy and terrorism are certainly real, they are hardly the most pressing security concerns. According to the 2013 *Human Development Report*, published annually by the United Nations Development Program, 65.6 percent of the Somali population lives in severe multidimensional poverty. (The Multidimensional Poverty Index was developed in 2010 and measures poverty on the basis of education, health, and living standards.) Somali children can expect to complete only 2.4 years of total schooling, which is substantially lower than anywhere else in the world. The maternal mortality rate is 1000 deaths per 100,000 live births. Estonia's, by comparison, is 2. Somalia's infant mortality rate is equally high at 108 deaths per 1000 live births, while their mortality rate for children under the age of five is 180. In comparison, Iceland's rate for both indicators is 2. The adult mortality rate is also alarming at 350 for women and 382 for men. Switzerland, by contrast, is 43 for women and 74 for men. (This metric predicts the number of 15-year-olds who will die by

FIGURE 5.1   In an effort to build a more peaceful society, citizens in war-torn northern Uganda have been encouraged to "Say no to small arms and light weapons." This poster suggests that guns are the cause, and not the solution, to regional insecurity. Photograph by Alicia C. Decker, 2008.

the age of 60 per 1000 adults.) Although a new government was recently sworn into power, human security remains tenuous in Somalia. Until good governance and sustainable development become the norm, the state will continue to be the country's greatest security threat.

In the rest of the chapter we examine four distinct case studies that examine the complex relationship between democratization and human security. We begin by looking at the significant problem of corruption and the major threat it poses to Africa today. The next section considers famine as another equally problematic outcome of poor governance. We demonstrate that famine is not simply an environmental catastrophe but, instead, a logical outcome of weak states and rampant political insecurity. In the third case study we analyze sexual and gender-based violence as one of the most dangerous repercussions of hypermilitarism, often pursued in the name of national security. The last section explores some of the ways in which communities, both local and global, have utilized peacemaking, peacekeeping, and peacebuilding to foster and support larger democratization efforts.

CORRUPTION

One of the oft-cited yet most underexplained threats to good governance in postcolonial Africa is corruption. Generalizations about the corrupt nature of contemporary Africa abound, but aside from being blamed for the fragility of democratization in Africa, there is little discussion of how to quantify corruption and, more importantly, how to minimize or completely eradicate such activities. Economist Laurence Cockcroft (2012) identified key factors that allow corruption to occur, and his definition demonstrates why African states are particularly vulnerable. According to him, Africa's corruption stems from the following: the fact that the size of unrecorded economies (or informal sectors) allows space for corrupt activities to go untracked; the investment of political finance, money often gained through illicit or corrupt means, into the political process with the expectation that the investor will be compensated with political and economic favor; the powerful role of organized crime; artificial pricing of Africa's natural resources by national and international companies; and the movement of illegally acquired agricultural, mineral, and natural resources from the informal sector to the formal sector. By these markers, both Africans and foreigners play a role in creating an environment fertile for corrupt activities, from local to national and regional levels.

Corruption is part of daily life in many African countries, from petty exchanges between individuals to clandestine transfers of millions of dollars between governments and businesses. According to a 2002 African Union (AU) estimate, corruption causes financial loss of up to $150 billion per year across Africa. In the past few decades, African countries and international donors have increasingly acknowledged the financial and political costs of such rampant and large-scale corruption, but the solutions are difficult to design. In the 1990s several declarations and agendas were launched at the continental level, with corruption mentioned as a crucial challenge for African nations to tackle, yet corruption continued to persist. In 2003 the AU made the eradication of corruption a key priority by passing the African Union Convention on Preventing and Combating Corruption. The goal of this convention was to energize and standardize a process to eradicate corruption throughout Africa and included a discussion of punishments for those found guilty of the practice. In 2009 the AU created an Advisory Board on Corruption to monitor the application of the Convention on Corruption and to offer policies and strategies for combating the illicit practice. The AU's strong anti-corruption stance stems from its recognition that corruption is a major threat to good governance and a deterrent of economic growth and that African people bear the costs of these transgressions. To gain support and momentum in the fight against corruption, there is also a UN initiative that designated an "International Anti-Corruption Day in Africa."

African nations began tackling corruption with the advent of anti-corruption commissions. Such commissions are tasked with the goal of identifying major corruption activities and bringing the perpetrators to justice. High-profile cases, particularly against former leaders, link internal corruption to other African nations and beyond the continent. Zambia is currently preparing for a case against former president Rupiah Banda, who is accused of stealing over $11 million by using an oil contract with Nigeria's government to pay for his campaign costs and siphon into his son's bank account. Although Zambia and other countries use anti-corruption commissions to deter potential corruption and punish those found guilty of corrupt activities, the impact of these commissions is still unclear. The UN Economic Commission for Africa observed that the commissions are inherently subject to scrutiny or discontinuation because they are funded and monitored by the executive branch, so they are limited in the individuals they can investigate and are swayed by commission members' own political loyalties.

There is another angle in the discussion of corruption that points to cultural causes, which, if true, may mean that it is an even more difficult problem to eliminate. Historians Robert O. Collins and James M. Burns argue that what outsiders label as corruption is something much more complex in the African context. They concede that corruption is obviously a problem in Africa but believe that "much of the corruption identified by Western observers occurred because of the failure to establish a national identity that could claim a greater fidelity than lineage or 'tribe.' . . . Labeling the distribution of spoils of decolonization to these deep-seated identities as corruption obscures the important African historical roots of that phenomenon" (Collins and Burns, 2007, p. 372). Other scholars also push for a deeper examination of corruption as an issue of loyalty and identity and turn to precolonial tributary relationships as a tradition that included a rewards-based system. Regardless of the roots and cultural context of modern-day corruption, it is evident that if these illicit activities persist, Africans will continue to carry the burden of living in an insecure state where bribes, nepotism, and exploitation threaten to destabilize already fragile political and socio-economic conditions.

FAMINE AND FOOD (IN)SECURITY

Famines in Africa over the last thirty years serve as disturbing reminders of the continent's vulnerability to food insecurity. We often understand famine to be the result of an environmental crisis, usually drought, which results in failed crops and subsequent food shortages. But famine is a much more complex situation that goes beyond the scope of environmental challenges. Oxfam International defines famine as a "triple failure." First, there is a failure in the production of food, usually caused by environmental conditions. Second, as environmental crises such as drought kill off livestock assets, people experience a decrease in their purchasing power and thus are unable to procure food to replace the food they cannot grow. The third factor is the failure of governments and aid agencies to respond appropriately and in a timely manner to intensifying food insecurity. Famine, simply put, is not only caused by environmental crises but also by governments and international donors that are unable to intervene before vulnerable populations reach a critical point in malnutrition (Oxfam International, 2012). The UN World Food Programme established their own definition of famine as measured through human health consequences. They declare famine in cases where 30 percent of children are acutely malnourished, 20 percent of the population does not have regular access to food, and there are two deaths per 10,000 adults or four deaths per 10,000 children every day.

The Horn of Africa has a traumatic history of recurring famine during the last three decades. Some of the most iconic images of Africans to reach European and American audiences come from the Ethiopian famine of 1984–85 in which around 1 million people perished and several million were left impoverished and unhealthy. A period of decreased rainfall, combined with an ongoing civil war and the diversion of money and resources to the country's military, placed Ethiopians in a tenuous position and famine eventually swept through the northern highlands. In late 1984, journalists publicized the humanitarian crisis and sparked a massive international response that encouraged nongovernmental organizations, foreign governments, and celebrities to donate food, money, and medical supplies to try and minimize the human suffering in Ethiopia.

Although the international response to the Ethiopian famine in the mid-1980s was able to intervene and bring short-term relief to the beleaguered population, it became obvious from the magnitude of that crisis that there needed to be longer-term strategies in place to prepare the region for future droughts. Aid agencies implemented the Famine Early Warning Systems Network in order to better predict the threat of famine as a way to combat the problem before massive deaths ensued. Oxfam International's research reveals that Ethiopia and its neighboring countries are increasingly susceptible to more frequent droughts and famines. In the early twentieth century droughts occurred once every ten to fifteen years, but by the mid-1980s they occurred approximately every eight years. Recent trends show that now droughts occur with shorter intervals in between, with droughts recorded every couple of years. It is clear, then, that governments of states prone to drought must intensify their efforts to prepare for these catastrophes.

Despite the obvious need for governments to work at improving preventative measures to minimize the threat and impact of famine, it appears the countries that are most affected by drought are failing to do so. In their study of famine and food insecurity, Patrick Webb and Joachim von Braun observe that from 1983 to 1993, Ethiopians were particularly vulnerable to recurrent food insecurity because there were "three major droughts, one national famine, the escalation and culmination of a civil war, experiments in the wholesale relocation of villagers, drastic reversals in government policy and structural adjustments," and that these "upheavals have contributed to a depletion of households' assets and savings, declining labour productivity . . . and a continued reluctance among farmers to invest in land productivity enhancement" (1994, p. 3). The consequence of this ten-year period was that Ethiopians were in a more fragile economic position in the early 1990s than they were in the 1980s and that anywhere from 5 to 15 million people were close to succumbing to famine. It was not just the years of low rainfall that placed Ethiopians in such a tenuous position. The government was not only *not* helping to improve conditions but actually contributed to mass starvation by *not* putting systems in place to alleviate food shortages in years of low agricultural production.

More recently, Somalia's population has faced an uphill challenge in preparing for and surviving inevitable droughts. Its lack of a centralized government over the past twenty years fomented the prevalence of militia groups and warlords who hijack food and medical aid to provide for their supporters (an occurrence that also took place in Ethiopia and Eritrea in the 1980s), cutting off desperately needed supplies for an increasingly malnourished and vulnerable population. In 2009 al-Shabaab, a powerful militia group, banned food aid convoys from going into southern Somalia. If the Horn of Africa does not stabilize politically and develop solid economic and agrarian policies and practices to combat the pervasive threat of drought and subsequent famine, there will continue to be large-scale loss of human life, and food insecurity will continue to plague the region.

SEXUAL AND GENDER-BASED VIOLENCE

Although democratization has provided exciting new opportunities for African women, it has also introduced significant security challenges. Many governments have attempted to protect their nascent democracies through military means (i.e., the "national security approach"). Some scholars question whether these conventional approaches can actually lead to genuine security. Amina Mama and Margo Okazawa-Rey, for instance, suggest that "there is now evidence that, for all the good that they may do in vanquishing local military forces involved in conflicts, the very forces deployed to quell unrest and secure conflict areas become participants in the war economy. They are also implicated in abusing and exploiting women in ways that resemble the actions of the forces they are mandated to control" (Mama and Okazawa-Rey, 2012, p. 100). By institutionalizing fear and violence at all levels of society, military forces create and sustain insecurity, particularly among women. Nowhere is the disturbing relationship between militarism and gender-based insecurity more pronounced than in the Democratic Republic of the Congo (DRC), a country so mired by conflict that one senior UN official dubbed it the "rape capital of the world."[1]

Despite its name, the DRC is one of the least democratic places on earth. Its citizens have endured unimaginable violence and repression since the earliest days of colonial rule, in large part because of the country's vast mineral wealth. The most recent gender-based violence stems from a series of wars and internal conflicts that date back to the mid-1990s, when Laurent-Désiré Kabila and his rebel forces ousted the long-standing dictator, Mobutu Sésé Seko, from power. Since then, Congolese women have lived in fear. According to a recent study, between 1.69 and 1.8 million women aged 15 to 49 years have been raped (Peterman, Palermo, and Bredenkamp, 2011, p. 1063). Because these figures are based on reported rapes and do not include individuals below the age of 15 or above the age of 49, the rate of sexual assault is likely to be significantly higher. Much of the violence has been committed by paramilitary personnel and soldiers. Men from local communities have also joined the military on raids so that they would be able to assault women without fear of punishment. In addition, UN peacekeepers have been responsible for raping women and/or forcing them into exploitative sexual relationships. Less visible, but also highly prevalent, is intimate partner sexual violence. Thirty-five percent of women in the DRC reported this type of violence, while the rate was "only" 12 percent in neighboring Rwanda (Peterman, Palermo, and Bredenkamp, 2011, p. 1065). Although Article 15 of the constitution stipulates that "public authorities are responsible for the elimination of sexual violence used as an instrument in the destabilization and displacement of families," marital rape is not illegal in the DRC. For most Congolese women, then, genuine democratization—that which includes the right to sexual autonomy, bodily integrity, and freedom from violence—remains nothing but a dream.

---

[1] BBC News. "UN Official Calls DR Congo 'Rape Capital of the World.'" April 28, 2010.

In an effort to combat these staggeringly high rates of gender-based violence, the UN Security Council has adopted a number of resolutions that promote peace and security for women. Resolution 1325, which was adopted on October 31, 2000, was the Security Council's first legal document to require parties involved in a conflict to respect women's rights and to support their participation in peace negotiations and postconflict reconstruction. The resolution "calls on all parties to armed conflict to take special measures to protect women and girls from gender-based violence, particularly rape and other forms of sexual abuse, and all other forms of violence in situations of armed conflict" (Article 10). It also emphasizes the responsibility of all States "to put an end to impunity and to prosecute those responsible for genocide, crimes against humanity, and war crimes including those relating to sexual and other violence against women and girls, and in this regard stresses the need to exclude these crimes, where feasible from amnesty provisions" (Article 11). In a ten-year impact assessment of the resolution, researchers found that widespread sexual and gender-based violence had remained a "formidable challenge" for peacekeeping missions and that it continued to be utilized as a deliberate strategy of conflict (United Nations, 2010, p. 10).

On June 19, 2008, the Security Council adopted Resolution 1820, which focuses exclusively on sexual violence in situations of armed conflict. It recognizes that "sexual violence, when used or commissioned as a tactic of war in order to deliberately target civilians or as a part of a widespread or systematic attack against civilian populations, can significantly exacerbate situations of armed conflict and may impede the restoration of international peace and security" (Article 1). It also notes that since "rape and other forms of sexual violence can constitute a war crime, a crime against humanity, or a constitutive act with respect to genocide," postconflict amnesty provisions must exclude sexual violence crimes (Article 4). The following year, they adopted Resolution 1888 as a follow-up to Resolution 1820 and Resolution 1889 as a follow-up to Resolution 1325. Most recently, in December 2010, they adopted Resolution 1960, which creates the institutional tools necessary to combat impunity and outlines the specific steps that are needed for the prevention of and protection from sexual violence in conflict. These resolutions provide a framework that offers protection to women, like those in the DRC, who so desperately need it. If democratization is going to be meaningful for African women, then their governments must embrace human security and not simply the "national security approach."

PEACEMAKING, PEACEKEEPING, AND PEACEBUILDING

Democratization is a process that is multidirectional, meaning that it can progress, stagnate, or retreat at different times depending on larger political circumstances. Over the last three decades, various armed conflicts have derailed democratic impulses and institutions within Africa. It is for this reason that serious attention must be paid to peacemaking, peacekeeping, and peacebuilding efforts, since they represent valuable opportunities to reinvigorate democratic growth. Peacemaking is a process that enables hostile parties to forge a settlement through diplomatic means. This can be accomplished through direct bilateral negotiations or with the assistance of a third-party mediator who helps both sides to communicate effectively so that they can draft a workable peace accord. One of the continent's most inspiring peacemaking initiatives is the Women's Mass Action for Peace Campaign, which was established by Liberian women in an effort to end the country's second civil war. What had begun as a small Christian prayer group in March 2003 quickly morphed into a large interfaith network of highly organized peace activists. Wearing all white and carrying banners that read, "The women of Liberia want peace now," the activists protested for several months, ultimately convincing the president and the rebel leaders to engage in peace talks. They traveled to Ghana in early June of that year in order to be a visible presence throughout the negotiations. When a series of political crises nearly halted the discussions in mid-July, the women linked arms and surrounded the building, refusing to let the delegates leave until a settlement was reached. Once a peace agreement was finally signed in mid-August, the women returned home to Liberia. They then spent the next two years working with the government to organize peaceful democratic elections. When the Liberian people elected Ellen Johnson Sirleaf as president on November 23, 2005, the women concluded their mass action campaign. The Nobel Committee recognized the significance of their efforts by awarding Leymah Gbowee, the key organizer of the Campaign, and President Ellen Johnson Sirleaf with the Nobel Peace Prize in 2011.[2]

Peacekeeping refers to any number of activities that contribute to the furtherance of an established peace process. This can include

---

[2] Sirleaf and Gbowee shared the Nobel Peace Prize with Tawakkol Karman, a women's rights activist from Yemen.

FIGURE 5.2   One of the most powerful movements to come out of
Africa in the early twenty-first century was the activism of Liberian women
calling for peace and an end to their country's second civil war. Women
from various ethnic, religious, and class backgrounds banded together and
put pressure on the Liberian government, rebel forces, and the international
community to move forward with peace talks and disarmament plans.
This picture shows Liberian peace protesters at the American Embassy in
Monrovia. Photograph by Peewee Flomoku, 2003.

monitoring troop withdrawals from former conflict zones, supervis-
ing elections, or providing aid for reconstruction. At the conclusion to
the second Liberian civil war in 2003, for instance, the United Nations sent in a peacekeeping force to monitor the ceasefire agreement,
to support humanitarian activities, and to assist with national security reform. It consisted of 15,000 military personnel as well as 1,115
police officers. Today it has just over 8,000 uniformed personnel. The
UN Mission in Liberia is one of eight active peacekeeping operations
in Africa. The others are headquartered in Mali, Darfur (Sudan),
Abyei (Sudan), South Sudan, Ivory Coast, Democratic Republic of the
Congo, and Western Sahara. Regional bodies also supply troops for
peacekeeping efforts. In 1990 Anglophone members of the Economic

Community of West African States (ECOWAS) established a Monitoring Group (ECOMOG) to intervene in the first Liberian civil war. They were later deployed to Sierra Leone in 1997 and Guinea Bissau in 1999. They also briefly intervened in the second Liberian civil war in 2003 but were quickly replaced by the United Nations. The African Union has also deployed peacekeeping troops to Darfur and Somalia. Most recently they have been trying to develop five African Standby Forces, which would represent the northern, southern, eastern, western, and central regions. Although some regions have operational brigades that could serve as the basis for a Standby Force, the future of this initiative remains uncertain.

Finally, peacebuilding refers to the process of normalizing relations and reconciling differences between the citizenry and all warring factions. Transitional justice is an important aspect of peacebuilding. This refers to the judicial and nonjudicial measures that countries implement in order to redress the legacies of extreme violence and abuse. These include criminal prosecutions, truth commissions, reparations programs, and memorials. Often a government will utilize a variety of different strategies to build peace and heal the nation. The International Criminal Tribunal for Rwanda is one example of criminal prosecution. In November 1994, just four months after the genocide which resulted in the deaths of nearly 1 million people, the United Nations Security Council established this international court to try suspected perpetrators. The Tribunal issued their final substantive trial judgment in December 2012, and they expect to complete appellate proceedings by July 2015. Because the number of alleged perpetrators was so high, the Tribunal only focused on the "ring leaders," the so-called masterminds behind the genocide. The government of Rwanda therefore had to establish a parallel judicial system that could try the masses. The regular court system had tried fewer than 400 cases by 1999, which at that rate would have taken several centuries to clear the genocide caseload.[3] In an effort to relieve the backlog, in 2002 the state began trying suspects before community-based *gacaca* courts. By the time they completed their work in June 2012, nearly 2 million people had been tried in more than twelve thousand different courts.

Truth commissions are another important mechanism of transitional justice. They have been established across the continent in

---

[3] Tharcisse Karugarama. "After Such Horror, What Forgiveness? How Gacaca Forced Virtue Upon Us." *The East African*, June 16, 2012.

various countries such as Zimbabwe (1985), Uganda (1986), Chad (1990), Burundi (1995), Nigeria (1999), Sierra Leone (1999), and Liberia (2006). The South African Truth and Reconciliation Commission (1995), however, is perhaps the most well known. In addition to identifying the causes and nature of human rights violations committed during the apartheid era and providing amnesty to those who fully disclosed their involvement in politically motivated violence, commissioners sought to identify victims so that reparations could be paid. Reparations, both material and symbolic, can be an important peacebuilding mechanism. Memorials can also help communities build peace after conflict. The Kigali Genocide Memorial Center, for instance, was built on a site where over 250,000 bodies were buried. It commemorates those who died in the Rwandan genocide and serves as a place for people to mourn their loved ones. If democratization in Africa is to move forward in the years ahead and not simply stagnate or retreat, then peacemaking, peacekeeping, and peacebuilding processes must remain (or become) a crucial aspect of governance.

CONCLUSION

In 2009, after spending days in a hospital after her husband viciously attacked her with a broken glass bottle, a Zambian woman went to her local police station to report the violence. She sat down at a desk with multiple signs taped to it, and to the wall behind, reminding women that they were protected from domestic violence by state laws and cautioning men that beating their wives was illegal. Yet when she spoke to the officer assigned to her, he rebuked her demands to press charges, patronizingly telling her that she was letting the devil ruin her marriage if she was not willing to forgive her husband and make peace with him. He told her that there was not really much that he could do for her. That a police officer, well informed about women's legal rights to report their abusers, would suggest to a woman armed with a copy of the legal code relating to domestic violence, photographs of the crime scene and injuries, a witness list, and visible cuts and bruises that she was being hasty to report her husband and that the police could not intervene on her behalf is a clear indicator that women's security is still a long way from being achieved. Likewise, the fact that Africans must brace themselves for daily corruption and food shortages reminds us that security, or the lack thereof, is defined in different ways by different people and continues to plague Africa today. Although peacemaking and peacekeeping efforts as well as peacebuilding reconciliation tribunals help ease the way out of conflict for bruised and battered populations, it is quite obvious that security at personal, local, and national levels is still severely lacking on the continent. Many Africans and interested outside observers hope that democratization will minimize some of these major threats to security, as good governance trumps corruption, famine, and various forms of violence. However, it remains to be seen whether shifting political ideologies and practices will be powerful enough to effect change given these extreme challenges.

REFERENCES

Ake, Claude. *The Feasibility of Democracy in Nigeria*. Dakar, Senegal: CODESRIA, 2000.

Clarke, Yaliwe. "Security Sector Reform in Africa: A Lost Opportunity to Deconstruct Militarized Masculinities?" *Feminist Africa* 10 (2008): 49–66.

Clifton, Don. "Security and a Sustainable World." *Journal of Sustainable Development* 2, no. 3 (November 2009): 3–17.

Cockcroft, Laurence. *Global Corruption: Money, Power and Ethics in the Modern World*. Philadelphia: University of Pennsylvania Press, 2012.

Collins, Robert O., and James M. Burns. *A History of Sub-Saharan Africa*. Cambridge, U.K.: Cambridge University Press, 2007.

Fund for Peace. *The Failed States Index 2013*. Washington, D.C.: The Fund for Peace, 2013.

Gilbert, Erik, and Jonathan T. Reynolds. *Africa in World History: From Prehistory to the Present*. 3d ed. Boston: Pearson, 2012.

Mama, Amina, and Margo Okazawa-Rey. "Militarism, Conflict and Women's Activism in the Global Era: Challenges and Prospects for Women in Three West African Contexts." *Feminist Review* 101 (2012): 97–123.

Oxfam International. *Food Crisis in the Horn of Africa: Progress Report July 2011–July 2012*. Oxford: Oxfam International, 2012.

Peterman, Amber, Tia Palermo, and Caryn Bredenkamp. "Estimates and Determinants of Sexual Violence against Women in the Democratic Republic of Congo." *American Journal of Public Health* 101, no. 6 (June 2011): 1060–1067.

Rice, Susan. Testimony before the Sub-Committee on Africa of the Committee on International Relations, House of Representatives, 117th Congress, First Session, November 15, 2001.

United Nations. *Ten-Year Impact Study on Implementation of UN Security Council Resolution 1325 (2000) on Women, Peace and Security in Peacekeeping.* New York: United Nations, 2010.

United Nations Development Program. *Human Development Report 2013: Rise of the South: Human Progress in a Diverse World.* New York: United Nations, 2013.

United Nations Population Division. *World Urbanization Prospects: The 2011 Revision,* CD Rom Edition. New York: United Nations, 2012.

Webb, Patrick, and Joachim von Braun. *Famine and Food Security in Ethiopia: Lessons for Africa.* Chichester, N.Y.: John Wiley & Sons in collaboration with the International Food Policy Research Institute, 1994.

Williams, Paul D. "Thinking about Security in Africa." *International Affairs* 83, no. 6 (2007): 1021–1038.

World Health Organization and United Nations Children's Fund (WHO/UNICEF). *Progress on Sanitation and Drinking Water: 2013 Update.* Geneva: World Health Organization, 2013.

SUPPLEMENTAL READING/FILMS/WEBSITES

Adebajo, Adekeye. *Peacekeeping in Africa: From the Suez Crisis to the Sudan Conflicts.* Boulder, Colo.: Lynne Rienner Publishers, 2011.

Curtis, Devon, Gwinyayi A. Dzinesa, and Adekeye Adebajo. *Peacebuilding, Power, and Politics in Africa.* Cambridge, U.K.: Cambridge University Press, 2012.

de Waal, Alex. *Famine Crimes: Politics and the Disaster Relief Industry in Africa.* Bloomington: Indiana University Press, 2009.

Gbowee, Leymah. *Mighty Be Our Powers: How Sisterhood, Prayer, and Sex Changed a Nation at War.* New York: Beast Books, 2011.

Gourevitch, Phillip. *We Wish to Inform You That Tomorrow We Will Be Killed with Our Families: Stories from Rwanda.* New York: St. Martin's Press, 1998.

Green, December. *Gender Violence in Africa: African Women's Responses.* London: Palgrave Macmillan, 1999.

Guest, Robert. *The Shackled Continent: Power, Corruption, and African Lives.* London: Pan Macmillan, 2004.

Jackson, Lisa. *The Greatest Silence: Rape in the Congo,* DVD. Women Make Movies, 2007.

Peck, Raoul. *Sometimes in April,* DVD. HBO Films, 2005.

Reticker, Gini. *Pray the Devil Back to Hell,* DVD. Balcony Releasing, 2008.

Epilogue

Democracy, or Something Else?

The difficulty in discussing contemporary Africa is that there is no endpoint or resolution to many of the issues covered in this book. Likewise, problems that were pressing a decade ago may be replaced by a different critical challenge and might seem less important in the future. As we finished this text, the big headlines out of Africa were about Nelson Mandela's deteriorating health and U.S. President Barack Obama's visit to the continent. The stories and chatter generated out of these two topics return us implicitly and explicitly to the larger theme of democratization and Africa's future. Although stories change and new issues arise, what seems to steadfastly remain is the discussion of how democracy may (or may not) be the way forward for Africa.

Mandela will forever be associated with pushing forward a democratization agenda. Although the end of apartheid was a tormented and painful one for many, once the end was formalized, Mandela's peaceful election and impressive tenure as president demonstrated what is possible in Africa. His extraordinary decision to step down peacefully, even though his re-election was all but guaranteed, sent a strong message to other African leaders, many of whom were entering their second decade in power by using strong-arm methods of rule and denying or thwarting the electoral process. Yet that message, though oft-mentioned, has not resulted in measurable results. As journalists, scholars, and Africans mourn the life of someone not yet passed, they seem to be mourning the lost hope of what Mandela offered his country and the continent.[1] Although his influence proved to not effect the change many hoped it would, he is still hailed as a true African hero and serves as a subtle example to many of why democracy should be the goal for African countries.

While writers wax poetic about Mandela's leadership and offer an understated nod to the potential benefits of the democratization process under just presidents, President Obama's voice is much louder and more aggressively pro-democratization. He declared Senegal to be one of America's strongest partners in Africa because "It's moving in the right direction with reforms to deepen democratic institutions, and as more Africans across this continent stand up and demand governments that are accountable and serve the people, I believe Senegal can be a great example."[2] Yet many critics of Obama's relationship with African countries believe he is doing more harm than good and that his emphasis on democratization is really just part of his agenda to use Africa as a launch pad for U.S. military interests on the continent and the Middle East. By building up friendships with states following the democratization plan, the United States is intent on building up strategic positions to build U.S. global security. This may put African countries, even those identified by the outside as democratic partners, in the center of conflict between the United States and other countries. The effect that would have on Africa's own fragile political, economic, and social conditions could be devastating, placing Africa's security as secondary to that of the United States.

It is evident that there is much to consider when pushing democratization as the sole way forward for Africa. Although democracy continues to be a popular catchphrase used by Africans and citizens of the Global North alike, an increasing number of people believe that African states must seek stability and security on their own terms and that good governance may not be exclusive to democracy. We will continue to watch how Africa is democratized and, more crucially, how democratization is Africanized in the coming decades.

---

[1] Sadly Nelson Mandela passed away on December 5, 2013 at the age of 95. The world is now mourning the loss of a remarkable man and the tremendous hope that he inspired.

[2] BBC. "Obama Urges Gay Rights in Africa during Trip to Senegal." *BBC News*, June 27, 2013.

INDEX